HOW TO BE
SuccesSoul

A GUIDE TO RECONNECTING WITH YOUR SOUL

Vicky Paul

ISBN: 978-1-913479-32-9 (paperback)
ISBN: 978-1-913479-33-6 (ebook)

That Guy's House
20-22 Wenlock Road
London
England
N1 7GU
www.thatguyshouse.com

vickypaul.com

 @vickyjpaul

 @vickyjpaul

 @vickyjpaul

'We carry inside us the wonders we seek outside us.'

Rumi

TTP

Preface

How to be SuccesSoul® is a straight-talking, insightful, funny, heartfelt and activating guide to help you reconnect with your soul. It focuses on bringing you back to who you truly ARE rather than trying to force you into someone you are NOT.

Many of us have lost our way and don't know how to regain our identity – or reconnect with our soul. Perhaps we don't think we have the ability or the power to change our situation, believing that to feel more soul full (i.e. happy, at peace, content etc) we have to give up all the things we cling onto and hold dear (and we think make us feel full).

We live in a world that does not truly encourage individuality. Instead, we are persuaded to conform to society's norm and strive for a 'successful life' - success being the ability to reach a goal, achieve some form of recognition and/or attain material wealth. So much has been written about success and what that means to us, but is it often measured in terms of money in today's society. I believe this drive for success in whatever venture you chose focusses too much of our attention outward and leaves us feeling unbalanced and stressed – or disconnected and lost. This book is not about finding success by today's definition of the word, although that is often a side effect. It is about exploring and reconnecting with the origin of the word success and how we express that through our individuality.

individuality (n.)
1610s, 'the aggregate of **one's idiosyncrasies**'

idiosyncrasy (n.)
c. 1600, from French *idiosyncrasie*, from Latinized form of Greek *idiosynkrasia* 'a peculiar temperament,' from *idios* 'one's own' (see idiom) + *synkrasis* 'temperament, mixture of **personal characteristics**,'

*www.etymonline.com. *Throughout this book, I share the original meaning of certain words, such as the examples above. Etymology is the study of the origin of words and how their meanings have changed over the centuries.*

Humans created language as a way to make sense of the world around us and to communicate more effectively with each other. As an intuitive, I believe the original meaning of the word success: 'go near to' (when the outcome could be good or bad, it was still deemed a success), resides in our soul. We just have to know how to return to it. Through examples of my own spiritual journey, and with channelled wisdom from Spirit, *How to be SuccesSoul* is part-memoir, part-navigational guide to help you reconnect with the true meaning of the words that frame your reality. It reintroduces you to the energetic essence of who you truly are – your soul. This means that you can feel alive and vital in your body and become the person you were born to be.

How to be SuccesSoul explores the origin of words, spirituality, soul, alignment, truth, ownership, responsibility and, of course, success. It is for anyone who has ever felt lost, disconnected, trapped by the paradoxes in life or simply overwhelmed by the infinite possibility of what now? It is for those amongst us looking for more meaning and purpose in their lives.

My intention with this book is for it to be your companion, a humble guide on your spiritual journey. It is for the soul searchers, the seekers, those of you at the early stages of your spiritual journey who perhaps feel a little lost like I did. This is often an overwhelming process and a subject that is difficult to verbalise. With this in mind, because I found it helpful, I have referred to your soul, the Universe, Spirit and the ego as separate things. They are not, but I found it easier to understand what was happening within me when I had 'them and me' or an internal and an external separate understanding in my mind. I hope you do too.

Finally, please be advised that I am not a qualified psychologist or medical practitioner. I am an intuitive, energy worker and Soul Plan Practitioner and the ideas and process in this book are my experiences and thoughts. They are only being provided as general information. They are not to be considered medical or psychological advice or treatment. Furthermore, they do not constitute a warranty, guarantee or predication regarding the outcome of an individual using *How to be SuccesSoul* for any particular problem or issue.

Contents

Introduction

When I was first aware of the idea for this book, I was lost, and when I wrote this introduction, I still felt a little lost. Not all the time, and it wasn't all-consuming, (thanks to my hubby, friends, family, wee dog, WINE, laughter and exercise). However, at times I felt in desperate need of a soul compass, a spiritual satnav to help me 'turn right at the next exit' back onto the Vicky Paul highway.

If I'm honest with myself, and let's be clear here, honesty is the only reason I can write this book (and the only reason you are reading it), I had been lost or off course for a pretty long time. Maybe you can relate, or maybe this doesn't quite resonate with you, but I think I can safely say that most of us have felt lost at some point in our lives, wondered what it's all for or why we are here.

Many of us have pressed our face against the proverbial gutter a few times, picked ourselves up, drank a shit load of (insert alcoholic beverage of choice), cursed like a trooper, punched or screamed into a cushion so the neighbours can't hear us losing our shit, shouted at our loved ones, hidden in our rooms, tried to run away from it all, licked our wounds, sobbed at the wretchedness of ourselves and pleaded with any God who wasn't too busy to fix our miserable life. Many of us have taken a reality check, briefly compared our crappy existence to most of the global population living in abject misery, felt super guilty for being so bloody self-centred, then finally admitted that it's time to suck it up, grow a set and fight another day.

Just me?

I am going to give you a little insight into my story because that's the reason I wrote the book. Think of it as literary speed dating. It'll help set the scene, and explain where, or should I say who, this book came from. And don't worry if you're more of a Tinder kinda person, swipe right to page 1; I won't take it personally. You can always come back for another peep if you fancy.

I promise this is the condensed version of the bits n bobs in my life that brought me to this point; a budding writer with a story to share, a desire to have the words in this book rain down on you like a shower of love, to have the pages of this book activate your soul so that you too can feel the joy that is yours for the taking.

Too much?

Perhaps, but you get the gist. I want to help you feel better, and I know this book will do that because I have been there, and I feel *so* much better.

I have always followed my own path, ever since I was a child and had a vision about what I wanted to do with my life. These were probably considered pipedreams or childhood fantasies, but I knew from an early age what my life would look like when I grew up. As it turns out, those specific dreams never became my reality, but I'll get to that later. What I aim to express here was that I was pretty focussed on me and my own wee world. I was born pre-internet, pre-globalisation, pre-awareness of the impact that my carbon footprint had on the world. I figured this was the way everyone lived their lives, and it was normal, whatever normal is, so I never really questioned it before now. Sure, many of us feel compelled to help others either through charity work or volunteering etc. You may even sign up to a regular thing like coaching a youth football team or teaching primary school kids' music or sharing words of wisdom on your blog or Instagram. However, generally speaking, most of us focus on ourselves, our family and friends, our immediate sphere of influence. Our own wee world.

I am not sure what changed or even when exactly, but the moment the idea for this book came to me, I wanted to share it with as many people as I could. Despite being considered an extrovert, I am quite private, so it has come as a surprise to me that I have been so willing to not only share my story in all its raw glory but share my relationship with Spirit in such a public fashion. I could not have done this ten years ago. However, moving through my own SuccesSoul journey over the last few years has resulted in a new-found level of self-acceptance, trust and a realisation that sharing our stories is the best way for us all to heal and move forward in our lives.

Well, what has changed, and why am I so keen to help as many people outside my immediate sphere? Spirit is the first reason. I trust my relationship with Spirit, and I know I would not be guided to do anything that was not for my highest good. I have spent a long time exploring different ways to improve myself and my experience on this planet, and I can honestly say that the guidance in this book is what got me to where I am today. I was also told by Spirit that I had to 'let the truth be known'. When I first 'heard' this, I was confused. It felt too vague because as far as I was concerned, there was no 'one' truth; there were billions of truths. I now understand that it was about sharing my truth, and in doing so, others (you) might live their (your) truth. The other reason for feeling this way is a genuine desire to make a difference, to help you reconnect with the very essence of who you are and take full and complete ownership of that. As a child who was bullied in school, I shied away from the very gifts that made me different and spent much of my teenage years trying to fit in and follow everyone else's path. Perhaps this is why I didn't manifest those childhood visions exactly as they appeared to me at the time. Perhaps they were simply childhood fantasies. Either way, it doesn't matter because I've found myself writing this book, and I was always meant to do that. Bullies or not, it's all gravy ☺.

It is the sum of my life experiences so far that have brought me to where I am now. They have inspired and fuelled my mission to help other souls activate Universal energy so that it flows freely, and you feel alive and vital in your body. I am passionate about raising the vibrational energy of this wonderful planet and supporting you to become who you were born to be. All I ask is that you keep an open mind, and the rest will take care of itself.

Section 1

The Understanding

This section sets the scene and helps you understand why you feel the way you do, why you are reading this book and what you need to know before you move onto the next stage of the book.

Chapter 1

I Saw My Papa

I saw my papa (grandfather) in my sitting room one night. He was standing in front of me, smiling and holding out his hand, inviting me to join him. At the time, he had been dead for nearly 25 years.

I remember that night as if it was yesterday. Anyone who knows me will think this unusual, as I am not known for my memory recall! He looked like a life-size 3D printed statue, clear like solid water, (ice has a bluey/green tinge to it, my papa didn't), and while he wasn't moving around, he was not static either. It felt like he was alive, just standing there like a regular human being, fully clothed in the cords, shirt and tweed jacket I remember him wearing as a child, with one exception. He was see-through. I was aware of the area behind him being out of focus as if his energy had blurred the wall. I wasn't alone, but I had just poured myself and my sister a large glass (is there any other size ☺) of Shiraz. I hadn't at that point made a dent in the drink, so I was **Stone. Cold. Sober.**

My sister had popped down for a visit. She lived two floors above me at the time, and we used to catch up regularly. We were sitting on our linen three-seater sofa. I had just dyed the covers black to jazz the place up a bit, and I remember thinking thank God I changed them from beige because she'd likely spill her glass of red if I told her what I'd seen. We were facing each other, chilling with our backs on the arms on the sofa. There was some sort of ambient music on in the background, and I was feeling in a good place having had an energy balancing session with a wonderful Swedish Wizard (her words not mine) called Jessica Vesterlund a few days before my sister's visit. I was still high from that and excited to tell her all about it.

When my papa appeared, it happened very quickly. One minute he was there and the next he was gone. He wasn't standing in the room for a long time, maybe five or ten seconds, but it felt like one of those moments in a movie when time stands still. It was long enough for me to *see* him and take it all in. He never spoke or made a sound or moved about, but his face was warm and loving, and he was smiling at me. I took this all in while talking to my sister, (you know how women like to multitask!). I don't know why, but I didn't share any of what I'd seen with her until much later. I presume I didn't want her to think I was a total looper, (no offence intended – PC box ticked, phew), or waste a good glass of wine.

I'd been having feelings that he was around me for the last couple of years, so it wasn't a total shock when I saw him. However, to the best of my knowledge, this was the first time I'd seen a dead person. The only other time I'd had a similar experience was when I was a child, and my other papa died. That happened very suddenly, (he was in a car accident), and someone's head and shoulders appeared outside our bedroom window. We were on the first floor. I put that experience down to an over-active imagination and left it at that. I knew that my papa appearing in my sitting room that night with my sister had nothing to do with a fertile imagination, and I was determined to explore it further.

In the years leading up to the visit from my papa, my face was pressed against the proverbial gutter. I was living and working in Belfast, and life wasn't great. I was lonely in a new city, up at 4 am to work early shifts on a local radio which I loved but spent every day and evening on my own once I'd finished work. I was tired and suffering from insomnia and tinnitus, which just made everything worse. When I was making my breakfast one morning, burst with lack of sleep, I loaded the spoon with coffee and instead of pouring the granules into the mug of steaming hot water, I hit it off the mug and spilt the coffee and hot water all over the kitchen worktop. Once I cleaned this all up and made a fresh mug, I decided to pour myself a bowl of cereal. I placed the bowl and the spoon on the wooden worktop, took the milk carton out the fridge and lifted the box of cereal. Mrs Clumsy no more, or so I thought. I opened the cereal box, and instead of tipping it to let the muesli fall out into the bowl, the box flipped out my hand. I didn't drop the box; it popped up and out of my hand. It was not a good morning, I can tell you. This was the first of many similar incidents, and every time they happened, it came into my head that it was my papa trying to get my attention, not fatigue or clumsiness.

Fast forward a few years to my flat in Glasgow (the one where my papa appeared). My then-boyfriend (now husband) had moved in, and we had decided to rearrange the furniture in the sitting-room to make space for his stuff. We moved the sofa 90 degrees from its original position so that it was perpendicular to the sitting room door. Previously we'd sat with our backs to the door looking straight out the window. I'm sure the Feng Shui experts will have something to say about the layout, but it felt right to us.

Following this reshuffle, when I sat on the sofa watching the TV, I could see the window out of the corner of my right eye and the sitting-room door out of the corner of my left eye. This detail is important because peripheral vision is good at detecting motion. Who knew? I thought all the motion was happening straight in front of me on the box.

Anyway, I started to see a black shadow out of the corner of my left eye when we were watching the TV, and sometimes it caught my attention out the corner of my right eye as a reflection on the window when it was dark outside. This went on for several months before I plucked up the courage to mention it to my boyfriend. To my utter surprise, he had been seeing the same thing too but thought nothing of it. We agreed that it must have been a car, a shadow from the street, or movement in the building opposite and said no more about it. Secretly, I still felt it was my papa.

Several months later, when I was at the energy session with Jessica, I plucked up the courage to ask her if my papa was visiting the flat. If there was anyone I could speak to about this kind of thing, it was her. She nodded and said my papa was curious to know who the man was that had moved in, as they both played the violin. Jessica didn't have any prior knowledge that either of them played the fiddle, and this was all I needed to know that I wasn't losing my mind. **I. Was. Buzzing.** An intense feeling of excitement and anticipation spread through my body and over my skin. I felt it flush my neck and face. My heart seemed to pound a little firmer in my chest, and like a wound-up toy ready to spin erratically across the floor, I was desperate to see where these sightings might lead.

My papa appeared a few days after this, as I was telling my sister about the session. Sadly, he has not physically appeared to me since, no matter how hard I try to manifest him. I have felt his presence on many occasions, sensed his familiar smell like a wooden dresser, shaving foam and worn wool, and can see his face up close in my mind's eye, but not in any room in front of me. Although I long to see him again, I got used to the fact that he might never reappear because I know that he came for a very specific reason. He got me back onto my creative, intuitive path. That 3D vision changed my life and was the reason I chose to explore my mediumship and psychic gifts and was guided to become a creative again and share my story.

As a kid, I was always drawing and making things. My papa was an artist and good with his hands too, and I used to spend hours at his writing bureau drawing with his pencils and pens. Before my papa passed away in hospital, the nurses removed his false teeth and his face collapsed in like *The Scream* by Edvard Munch. The night he died, I came home from the hospital after saying my goodbyes and drew *The Scream* over and over. It was the last time I painted until my papa came through to me in Belfast. I believe he was trying to get me to paint and create again as a means of exploring and understanding my psychic and mediumship gifts. Intuitive painting helps access our highest wisdom by connecting to our deep, inner, true creative nature: our soul self.

Chapter 2

Success

For most of us, success is the ability to reach a goal, achieve some form of recognition and/or attain material wealth. This is shaped by modern society and, unfortunately, perpetuates a state of fear. *How to be SuccesSoul* is not a how-to manual for being successful in the modern sense of the word, although that is often a side effect of this journey. It is about success in the original sense of the word.

Like so much of our language, the original definition of success has changed over the centuries, and it started life as a completely different story. I believe that story, the energetic footprint of the original meaning, still resides within us. All we have to do is access it by reframing the way we feel about it.

> **Success** is the noun form of the verb to 'succeed', which comes from the Latin *succedere*: meaning to 'go under, go up, come close after, **go near to**'. Citations begin appearing around 1535 - focussed

7

on the 'what comes next/result' aspect of the word; the idea that the result was positive, i.e. 'successful' in the modern sense, was irrelevant - an outcome could be good or bad, it was still 'a success'.

SuccesSoul, as a definition is the result or consequence of 'going near to' our soul, of reconnecting with our soul self. We are already a success just by being here on this planet, a soul in a human body. How powerful is that statement? I believe that the evolving meanings of the words we use shape our past, present and future. By reminding ourselves of the energetic essence of the words that define our experiences, we have the power to transform our lives.

Success is a such a fickle word; it's inspiring, crushing, elusive, scary, out of reach and everything else in-between. We are obsessed with success, yet mostly, in our eyes, we fail to achieve it. We strive for it throughout our lives and use it as a measure to benchmark ourselves against each other, not to mention berate and belittle ourselves for not achieving it.

What is it about success that has us locked and loaded in its grip?

So much has been written about success and what it means to us personally and collectively. However, it is more often than not measured in terms of money in today's society. There is, like everything in this world, a cost to achieving success, and as hard as it is to be successful, it's even harder to keep it. The drive for success causes wars. It causes relationships to break up, ill health and a lifetime of never being or having enough. Despite these obvious and very well-known pitfalls, we still find ourselves hypnotised by its spell. From a young age, we are taught about success in school, and we are encouraged to work hard to give us the best chance of achieving it. The media is full of images of successful people, and thanks to reality TV, mere mortals can have their fifteen minutes of it. The truth is that our obsession with success in whatever venture we chose focusses too much of our attention outward and leaves us unbalanced and stressed, disconnected and lost.

Are we deluded in thinking that it's the answer to all our problems, the giver of life, the creator of dreams, the holy grail of happiness? If so, why does it remain elusive for so many of us?

The first problem with success is that one size does not fit all. From our early years, we are encouraged to fit in, to act and be a certain way. Very quickly, we realise that certain characteristics or personality traits are deemed more attractive, and we try to change or mask our unique characteristics in order to avoid being singled out or to ensure we are accepted. In a world where we are hell-bent on making everyone the same, the current definition of success is not achievable for a great many of us.

Despite our grasp of language and our ability to verbally express ourselves, it helps to reconsider the origin of the words we use. I believe their original meaning still resides in our soul, and we carry that knowing through many lifetimes despite the changes that take place in our language over the generations. When we reconnect with our ancestor's definition, our present understanding of the word takes on a whole new meaning – it seems to move from a knowing in our brain to an understanding in our bodies that feels like an expansion of consciousness.

The problem with success is that the meaning of the word, and for that matter a considerable amount of our language, has morphed over the centuries to mean something different to what it did all those centuries ago. 'Going under', for example, would not be considered a success by today's standards.

I believe, or perhaps more accurately I have been guided to know, that the original meaning of the words our ancestors created, like success, resides in our soul DNA. Biological DNA is acquired from our birth parents; soul DNA is our energetic imprint and history across lifetimes. We can share our soul DNA with individuals called 'soul groups', experiencing lifetimes together. Soul groups are less likely to be biological family. They are our soul sisters and brothers, the people you meet and just *know*.

Soul DNA needs to be activated for us to connect with the vibrational frequencies of information and awareness that reside in us and can guide us in this lifetime. But it often stays dormant until we are ready to follow our spiritual path. Most people devote the first part of their lives to living a worldly or human experience, exploring and connecting to the world through the physical senses like touch, taste and smell. We are in our body and mind, often unaware of the spiritual aspect of our being. It's not until we reach a point in our life when we start to feel lost, or the shit hits the fan, or we just need more meaning, that we recognise there must be more to us than the physical aspects.

Soul reconnection is the process of awakening and activating our spiritual potential. It is a process of unfolding, opening up, letting go and remembering that we are more than our physical bodies. We are born fully aware that we are body, mind and soul. Both an inward and outward being. Our ego is the conscious aspect of our being and tricks us into ignoring our soul or source energy. By telling our ego to back off, we are able to access our soul stories and the language in our soul DNA that can assist our Spiritual Awakening, or soul reconnection, in this lifetime. Think of it like the fast track queue at airport security. You get to pass through scanners, head to duty-free and start your holiday much quicker and in a better mood. Pretty amazing stuff, isn't it?

Before I started on my own SuccesSoul journey, success meant pretty much the same to me as it did/does to you. I benchmarked myself against my peers and spent a huge amount of time and energy striving for financial security, a dream career and the perfect home, (cars not so much, but that's just me ☺) – that said I am still a home bird and love nesting, interior decorating and home comforts. Anyway, it was around the time that my papa appeared that I started to learn about the law of attraction, and in particular, the author, Louise Hay. For those not familiar with the law of attraction, it's the theory that everything is energy and therefore we attract into our lives that which we are focussing on. Well, knock me over with a feather. All that worry about achieving success, financial security and the perfect home only brought me more worry, financial stress and house disasters. More on the house disasters later. The session I had with Jessica just before my papa's visit was another turning point for me. I felt in my whole being, physical and spiritual, just how potent the invisible (or unseen) aspects of our lives are. It inspired me to understand and unearth everything I could about energy and our ability to work with it, harness it, and in some cases, influence it. During our time together, Jessica also suggested I repeat the sentence 'I am safe, I am secure, I have no lack.' This was really the beginning of my journey to understanding that what we think and say shapes our reality and was the reason I chose to look more closely at words and language.

There are so many words in our vocabulary today that mean something completely different than they used to. This contradiction creates a conflict between what our soul understands the meaning of a word to be, and what the brain defines it as. This lexiconflict, (new word), causes friction between our biological and soul DNA, which results in confusion and an inability to connect the dots. If left unchecked, this confusion can manifest itself as emotional outbursts.

The words you use (in thought or speech) create your past, present and future. They shape your reality and have the power to bring abundance or scarcity into your life. Affirmations are the practice of positive thinking and verbal self-empowerment to help you overcome negative thought patterns and behaviours. Based on the theory that we are what we think, everything we think and say is really an affirmation. They are big business, and you've no doubt come across them all over social media.

affirmation (n.)
early 15c, 'assertion that something is true,' from
Old French *afermacion* 'confirmation' (14c.), from
Latin *affirmationem* (nominative *affirmatio*) 'an
affirmation, solid assurance,' noun of action from
past-participle stem of *affirmare* '**to make steady;
strengthen; confirm**,'

The first step to embracing affirmations is to become
aware of what you are actually saying. When I started
this, I couldn't believe how negative I was. I said 'no' a lot
and used the words *problem, can't* and *won't* all the time.
How often do you say you're tired, or always running late,
or never have enough time, are too fat, too thin or not fit
enough? These are all affirmations, but clearly not the
ones you want to be using!

The second step, and the main thrust in affirmations
working, is realising that the Universe pays attention to
the energy behind the words and not just the words.
There is NO point saying 'I feel great' if you feel like a
bag of shit! There are a couple of 'rules' to using
affirmations.

1. Positive affirmations are always in the present
    tense. Don't use 'will' 'used to' or 'going to'.

2. An obvious one, but positive affirmations only
    use positive words so no more 'don't' 'can't' or
    'won't'.

3. Positive affirmations are factual statements.
    These are the truth, which means 'might' and
    'could' are off the table.

4. Repetition is key. Saying something once and expecting a miracle ain't gonna work.

5. It can be tricky to say something if it feels like a lie. 'I love my body' is a prime example. Start off small: 'I can get fit' or 'I can lose weight', as this doesn't make it feel *false*.

6. You have to *feel* the affirmation for it to work. You can use physical touch to help you feel into it. Rub your hands or hold your hand over your heart.

Here are a few affirmations to get you started. There are thousands all over the internet, so have a dig until you find something that feels right for you and what you want to achieve.

> I know, accept and am true to myself.
> I eat well, exercise regularly and get plenty of rest.
> I enjoy my life.
> I am loving and lovable.
> I have plenty of energy.
> I have a fulfilling career.
> I have great work-life balance.
> I make decisions easily.
> I see others as good people who are trying their best.

Despite there being a number of different versions of success in the world today, there is still no universal measure. It should be based on whether or not your actions reflect your beliefs, and your effort is enough to achieve your goals.

A consumer culture tremendously biases the notion of success - it heavily favours the goal of individual success over group/community success. It favours the concentration of wealth over the distribution of wealth. It favours the exploitation of the environment over the preservation of it. It favours one-upmanship over the idea that a rising tide lifts all boats.

I'd like you to take some time to ponder the following question and then analyse your answer. Write down as many reasons as you can for each – and for this to really be of use to you, please be honest. You can tear it up and throw it away afterwards if you are surprised by your answer.

Of these two people, who best represents success to you? You can only pick one name, and I would like you to write down the reasons for your choice. There is no right or wrong answer. This exercise is to connect you with the definition of success as you believe it to be.

Mark Zuckerberg – the American internet entrepreneur who co-founded Facebook. He set up the social networking site from his dorm room at Harvard University, then dropped out a year later to devote himself to it full time. In the 18 years since it started, Facebook is now worth $512 billion (according to the company's market capitalisation), and he is personally worth $80.7 billion (January 2020).

OR

Mother Teresa – born Agnes Bojaxhiu to Albanian parents living under the Ottoman Empire. She trained as a nun and moved to India in 1929 to build a missionary in Calcutta. She was a healer and devoted her life to caring for the sick, destitute and poor and won the Nobel Peace Prize in 1979. She was made a Saint in 2016.

_____

_____

_____

_____

_____

_____

_____

_____

_____

_____

_____

Who did you pick as the most successful person between Mark Zuckerberg or Mother Teresa? According to TIME Magazine, the answer was both:

Mark Zuckerberg was one of their most influential people in 2019.

Mother Teresa was one of their 25 most powerful women of the past century.

Very often the people we would consider successful, and who have been driven to achieve the modern definition of success – that is wealth and fame - on attaining it, do not consider those things to be achievements or the reasons they feel accomplished. Billionaire, Richard Branson, believes success is about happiness. Huffington Post co-founder, Arianna Huffington, says that money and power aren't enough: wellbeing, wisdom, wonder and giving also matter. Acclaimed author, Maya Angelou, believed success is liking yourself, liking what you do and liking how you do it. Why is it then that these high achievers all feel this way? Maybe it's because following a lifetime of striving, achieving for and gaining material success, they realised it wasn't what they were looking for.

If you take the definition of success at face value, and in its current form, the reality is that most of us are doomed to fail. However, if you are open to the idea of going back to the original meaning of the word success – that is 'go near to' – then you open yourself up to a whole new level of possibility.

There are a number of rich and famous people who embodied the original meaning of the word success, whether they knew it or not at the time, and in doing so inadvertently achieved the modern version of it. Jim Carrey lived in a VW bus and in a tent on his sister's lawn because he was in financial difficulty. This was where he developed his sense of humour. Halle Berry moved to New York because she knew in her soul that she wanted to be an actress. She was so committed to this belief, that when she ran out of money she didn't give up and head home, she moved into a homeless shelter and credits the whole experience to teaching her how to take care of herself. On a similar vein, Daniel Craig, aka 007, was so committed to being an actor that he waited on tables and slept on park benches in his early career. Multi-platinum recording artist Jewel lived on the streets for a year after her boss fired her. She wrote songs, started singing in a local café and ended up securing a label deal. Jewel has since sold in excess of 30 million albums worldwide. While these are considered rags to riches stories, they are also SuccesSoul stories. These people were so true to their soul's calling that they were prepared to endure extreme hardship in pursuit of their life purpose.

Chapter 3

You Are Not Losing Your Mind

Now that you are aware of the original meaning of the word success, Chapter 3 is the beginning of your SuccesSoul journey. It is the point in your life when the call to transform begins to surface enough for you to sit back and take notice.

There are signs that manifest physically, emotionally, mentally or spiritually within us when we are having a realisation. A realisation is the slow deep-rooted recognition that we are a soul in a human body. Energy, consciousness, love and light. This is different from our ego, or our ego-mind.

Our ego-mind is thoughts and beliefs, but it is also emotions, memories, visual images, and it has a life of its own. Our ego-mind sees things for what they're pretending to be, while our soul always sees them as they are. Our ego-mind fights this realisation or tries to control it, and the battle can go on for years. It is usually at this stage in our lives that we start to experience feeling lost, unsatisfied and that there is more to life than work, clothes, drinking etc. We are searching for meaning and purpose. We may have picked up a few bad habits or addictions along the way to help mask our realisation, and our awareness of these bad habits or addictions is usually accompanied by guilt. To offer some clarity at this stage in your realignment, I have included a symptom checker at the end of this chapter, (everybody loves to Google their symptoms!). It is a list of signs that you might be experiencing as part of your realisation and an explanation of how they might manifest.

Perhaps you know that there is something more to your life, but you can't quite put your finger on it; you feel dissatisfied with how things have turned out, or you are not where you thought you would be at this stage in your life, or you have habits that are not serving your highest good, but you are struggling to let them go, or you have had a life-changing moment that has knocked you for six and left you disillusioned, or you have had some sort of calling to lead a higher purpose.

All of these reasons are a sign that your soul is calling you to remember who you are. We often live the first part of our life in the worldly aspect, that is as a human being with a soul. At some stage, usually as an adult, and after a bit of 'living', we begin to sense that we are more than the body and mind we inhabit. We are starting to become more aware of our spiritual being - we are after all a soul with a body rather than a body with a soul. This distinction becomes even more important to us as we are called to explore a deeper connection and meaning in our lives. In its broadest sense, this process is called a Spiritual Awakening, and it is not a conscious decision. We do not wake up one morning and decide to awaken, seek truth, have a revelation, breakthrough or chose to go on the hunt for enlightenment. We cannot make ourselves have a Spiritual Awakening; it happens to us, for us, by us and only when we are in the right energy to receive the lessons and learnings that are part of our awakening.

SPOILER ALERT

The Spiritual Awakening process isn't all love, light, flowers, candles, incense, rituals, shrines and crystals.

In my experience, and in the case of those I have spoken to, a Spiritual Awakening turns your entire life upside down and inside out. It feels relentless, isolating, lonely and without end. It is not a choice any sane person would make, which is why when you start to experience the symptoms or become aware of the signs, you think you are losing your mind. So many people, including me, don't pay attention to the signs until we are forced to. This is how my Spiritual Awakening happened.

I was in my mid-thirties, living the dream as an award-winning radio presenter and had just bought a gorgeous house with my boyfriend at the time. Life was good. I woke up one Friday, went to work at 5 am, got sacked at 9.55 am and was asked to leave the building by 10.10 am. To add insult to injury, the boss sent an email around the entire office congratulating the new presenter, who was taking over from me on Monday, before I'd had the chance to clear my desk and exit the building.

Talk. About. Humiliating. It was public, it felt personal, and I wanted to shrink away from my feelings of rejection, shame and anger. The fall out took me to rock bottom, with my physical and emotional health suffering. My relationship ended, and we sold our house. I lost colleagues I thought were friends. I spent a chunk of my savings supporting myself through unemployment, and I ended up moving in with a friend because the house I bought myself had damp, and the sale fell through a couple of days before I was due to pick up the keys. As painful as this experience was, it transformed my life. I rediscovered my ability to sense and work with energy and to communicate with Spirit. I was guided to start painting again as a way of communicating Universal energy. It made me passionate about self-realisation, transformation and soul reconnection and is the reason I have written this book. It knocked me (rather brutally) back on course.

When we lose something we hold dear, it can send us into freefall. We lose control of ourselves, our lives and sometimes our grip on reality.

> **lose (v.)**
> Old English *losian* 'be lost, **perish**,' from *los* 'destruction, loss,'

The truth is, a Spiritual Awakening does make you lose your mind – the old you perishes to make way for the real you.

Thankfully Spiritual Awakening is a much more accepted and openly talked about experience today than it was as little as twenty years ago, and there are so many wonderful websites and blogs covering the topic. Given the vast amount of information on the subject, you will soon realise that you are not going through this alone, even though you will feel alone when you are going through it. The Universe loves a contradiction.

What you will begin to realise is that these signs manifest physically, emotionally, mentally and spiritually to varying degrees of intensity and length. There are several key changes or transitions that take place during an awakening, so before picking up your smartphone to Google the signs (this need for immediacy is actually one of the signs), I have included a list at the end of this chapter. It is by no means exhaustive, but like any good online medical symptom checker (we've all played doctor, and self-diagnosed then freaked out when our symptoms suggest we've got something serious), this list is meant to help you understand what you are feeling and recognise some of the signs.

A footnote not quite at the foot of the page: A Spiritual Awakening does not unfold by learning or external guidance; it comes from within. Any list of signs will not fast track your experience, and it will not make it easier or more fun. It is meant to be like a good friend, a comfort and support in your time of need and there to let you know that you are not alone. Just like a good friend cannot prevent you from feeling the pain you experience when a relationship falls apart, this list cannot prevent you from experiencing the painful symptoms of your awakening.

In truth, your awakening is a reconnection, a process of self-discovery, of remembering who you truly are. It can happen fairly quickly, or it can last years (you have yourself to thank for that). It is not about being chosen, and it is not for the chosen few - please don't let social media fool you into thinking otherwise. It is both passive and active, requiring patience and commitment. Ok that last part, commitment, happens without your consent. Once you're on this journey, there is no stopping.

Not everyone has this experience as part of their life path, and many people have an awakening even though they were never in the least bit interested in anything spiritual.

Spirituality, and 'being spiritual' is met with a mixed reception, depending on your audience. There is no agreed-upon definition of spirituality because it means different things to different people. Some people call themselves spiritual even though they do not believe in, or communicate, with Spirit and some call themselves spiritual rather than religious, believing that they do not need a church, religious building (depending on your faith) or community to connect with a higher power. Some people consider themselves spiritual simply because they believe in ethical values like compassion and empathy towards each other. Spirituality can also be a set of practices that are comforting and healthy - yoga and tai chi, for example. Some people call themselves spiritual because they believe in the mystical sense that we are all connected to one another and the Universe. Being spiritual brings comfort when the shit hits the fan because people believe things happen for a reason. It does not matter what your personal definition of spirituality is, or even whether you call yourself spiritual or not, as humans we need to feel emotionally secure and to do that we need to reconnect with our feeling centre, our heart, our soul, our spirit, our essence.

Spiritual Awakening is non-negotiable if it is your soul's calling. Despite the upheaval, struggle and pain, it will transform your life for the better and do so in immeasurable ways. Hang in there. You got this; I promise.

Now that I have sold it to you ☺, here is the list. As I said before, it is not exhaustive, so I invite you to add your own signs and experiences at the end of this chapter and share them on social media and with your family and friends. The more we share our experiences, the more we are able to support each other. Who knows, you may even reconnect with one of your soul sisters or brothers in the process?

Signs you are not losing your mind and might be going through a Spiritual Awakening.

- You feel that something has changed inside you. Initially, this might be a sense of fear because deep down, you know changes are afoot, and that means certain things and people will go. But like the moth to the flame, you aim headlong into the light.
- You become aware of your negative thoughts, actions and habits. You change your language, stop shopping/boozing/eating to fill a hole and are super buzzed by this realisation.
- You increasingly want to spend time alone despite usually being the life and soul of the party. You will still connect with friends, but you

don't feel like a loser for being in on your own on a Saturday night.

- You can't stand superficiality or anything that is not authentic – this usually manifests in lots of unfriending and unfollowing. On that note, you'd be quite happy to give up social media altogether, and while you're at it, you stop watching shit on the TV.
- You have deep sadness and compassion about all the suffering in the world, and you want to do something to make this world a better place. This is when you want to jack it all in and build schools in Syria or campaign for no more plastic.
- A deep desire to understand your soul purpose, the reason you are actually on this planet.
- Hypersensitivity to light and noise and the full moon. Crystals, chakras and Angel/Goddess cards find their way into your life if they have not manifested already.
- An increase in creativity and the need to make your dreams a reality. Wanting to have a baby, finding a talent for art, baking and the desire for a hobby other than the gym/sport.
- A willingness to face up to the truth of who you are and the courage to live it. Taking ownership of all that you are, proud to be different and an individual, realising that you don't need validation for who you are.
- Increased intuition, coincidences and synchronicities on your life. You are opening up, and the Universe is blending with you to connect you to your higher purpose.

- More awareness of the food you eat and a desire to lay off the booze. You realise your body is a God-given miracle and it needs healthy nourishing food to flourish. You notice an increase in everything once you do stop eating shite and it's like a legal high – the more healthily you eat, the more buzzed you become.
- Changing sleep patterns. You need more or less, dream vividly, meet ancestors, learn lessons and fall into sleep more quickly with each day.
- One of my favourites – you stop worrying about things and notice a change in your attitude. I call this the 'Fuck It' phase! You are bold and brave and spontaneous and trusting. You have faith that life has got your back.
- Aversion to conflict of any kind – in your relationships, while you are driving or watching the TV.
- You stop judging yourselves and other people and check yourself when you do. You are only human after all, but it doesn't feel good when you do still judge.
- Increase in the desire to love and give. You realise there is more joy in giving and in turn you attract more love and giving.
- Strong connection with animals and the need to spend time in nature. You realise you are sometimes happier in the company of animals and nature than you are with people. Creatures are divine beings and to connect with them is to connect with pure source/Universal energy.
- Random moments of actual bliss for no apparent reason, and because you have already passed

the 'Fuck It' phase you don't care if you spontaneously burst into happiness at the bus stop.

Write down your own Spiritual Awakening signs below:

_____

_____

_____

_____

_____

_____

_____

_____

_____

_____

_____

_____

_____

_____

_____

Chapter 4

Wakey Wakey

For most people, a Spiritual Awakening follows a moment when you literally 'wake up' and realise that your perception and experience of the world around you has changed, or needs to change because you cannot carry on as you are.

Spiritual Awakening stirs the deepest and most significant questions within us that we have perhaps been unaware of, ignored or been too scared about to go there. Ignoring our soul's rumblings causes an imbalance that manifests in unhealthy choices and patterns of behaviour. We either try to silence the voice or believe we can shortcut the process to oneness/happiness by choosing external stimuli over internal investigation, hence the tendency towards extreme behaviours: too much food, booze, meaningless sex, drugs, exercise, shopping, photographing yourself for social media – whatever your vice of choice is. This is a futile exercise that only serves the powers that be who want you to live your life in a permanent state of fear so that you spend your money, and line their pockets, trying to make yourself feel safe/happy/one.

When we find ourselves at this stage, we question our lives and ourselves asking, 'What should I do?' Philosophers, however, have a different approach. They ask, 'What kind of person should I be?' Philosophers often turn to something called virtue ethics for answers to these life-changing questions.

> Virtue ethics is a broad term for theories that emphasise the role of character and virtue in moral philosophy rather than either doing one's duty or acting in order to bring about good consequences. *Internet Encyclopaedia of Philosophy*

Aristotle, one of the most influential philosophers of all time, developed a comprehensive system of virtue ethics that we can still learn from today.

> Plato, the Athenian philosopher during the Classical period in Ancient Greece (c.428-347 B.C), believed that knowledge is discovered in virtue (in Greek, *arete* meaning skill or excellence; in Latin, *virtus*), while ignorance is vice. Plato was a student of Socrates and later became the teacher of Aristotle. Plato and Aristotle talked a lot about virtue and vice. They came at it from similar places, but their ideas about virtue were different. Plato's philosophy was more about non-material things, like ideas

and love. Aristotle liked things that are more measurable and physical.

Stick with me here; there is a point to all this.

> In Aristotle's philosophy, virtue is a state of being. It could be understood as any positive sentiment that leads to the happiness of ourselves and others (the *good* qualities a person can possess as it were). Vice is simply the absence of virtue, that which does not lead to happiness (the things we generally consider *bad* qualities). With this in mind, it's no wonder we end up reaching for a vice when we chose not to discover knowledge (listen to our soul's rumblings) and do little to understand what happiness means to ourselves and others.

I told you we'd get there!

If you are still unsure whether your boozing, shopping, overeating and so on, is a vice or virtue, I would like you to take a look at Aristotle's Golden Mean Chart. It's a table he created to show the desirable middle ground (virtue) between two extremes (vices).

I have included an exercise on the next page called **Vice or Virtue**. Before you turn the page, please look at this table and consider each of the columns and the lists of vices and virtues. Do any of your behaviours, character traits or habits currently fall into either of the vice categories? Try to be honest with yourself. Turn the page when you are finished.

	SPHERE OF ACTION	Vice of Deficiency	Virtue	Vice of Excess
Divine Goods	Knowing	Ignorance	Wisdom	Sophistry
	Moderation	Abstention	Temperance	Indulgence
	Equality	Unfairness	Justice	Overly Fair
	Fear and Confidence	Cowardice	Courage	Rashness
Human Goods	Wellbeing	Unhealthy	Health	Overly Health Conscious
	Image	Too Humble	Beauty	Vanity
	Physical and Mental Shape	Weakness/ Fear	Strength	Over-compensation
	Wealth	Stinginess	Charity	Greed

Vice or Virtue Exercise

I would like you to make a list of anything in your life that falls into each of the three categories: Vice of Deficiency, Virtue and Vice of Excess.

This exercise is not meant to trouble or shame you; it's designed to bring your attention to any imbalances in your life based on your conscious behavioural choices. The real work comes when you accept that there is a more balanced way of living, and you actively choose to make the changes you need to create more balance.

Here's an excerpt from my exercise to use as an example and get you started.

	Sphere of Action	Vice of Deficiency	Virtue	Vice of Excess
Divine **Goods**	**Knowing** Wanted to learn more about philosophy for researching and writing this book.	**Ignorance** Couldn't be bothered going to the bookshop to buy a book. When I read some book synopsises on Amazon, I was overwhelmed by the information, decided I wasn't able to focus on or retain the information so didn't buy anything.	**Wisdom** Found a beginner's philosophy class and learned new concepts while meeting other people who were able to explain tricky concepts in a different way, thereby helping me understand more easily.	**Sophistry** Why was I trying to learn philosophy at this stage in my life? I had managed to get this far and never really needed more than a layman's knowledge. My book isn't a study of philosophy, so I don't need to learn anything new. It's a waste of my time.

Now it's your turn. If you need more space, then write out the columns on a separate piece of paper.

	SPHERE OF ACTION	Vice of Deficiency	Virtue	Vice of Excess
Divine Goods	Knowing	Ignorance	Wisdom	Sophistry
	Moderation	Abstention	Temperance	Indulgence
	Equality	Unfairness	Justice	Overly Fair
	Fear and Confidence	Cowardice	Courage	Rashness

Human Goods	Wellbeing	Unhealthy	Health	Overly Health Conscious
	Image	Too Humble	Beauty	Vanity
	Physical and Mental Shape	Weakness/ Fear	Strength	Over-compensation
	Wealth	Stinginess	Charity	Greed

Spiritual Awakening is an intense process that is rough for some and less so for others. It is not for the faint-hearted, but the brave of heart and true of soul. This journey of self-discovery will transform you irreversibly, bring you joy in ways you cannot imagine, and at times, fill you with a deep and inexplicable sadness. It's a rollercoaster people, but once you step off it and find yourself liberating a spider or a wasp, rather than squashing it, you will laugh and know you are forever anew.

An awakening can happen fairly quickly, like the person whose alarm goes off, reaches over, presses mute, has a stretch then gets up. For the rest of us, myself included, the alarm gets snoozed eight times, all staggered a few minutes apart, then you groggily drag yourself out of bed. Either way, it's personal to you, and that's one of the lessons we all have as part of this process: don't compare yourself to other people. Their journey takes whatever time it takes. You may be in the clapped-out banger this time around, and the other guy's in the sportscar. Let them pass, rest assured you'll pass each other further down the track when they've run out of fuel because they were driving too fast.

I didn't recognise one of my reawakening episodes until a few years into the whole process. Memories long hidden began to resurface and remind me that I was awake spiritually as a child. I have always known things about how people felt, why they said what they said, or did what they did. I predicted snow on a sunny day in late spring when I was six and knew that my papa died before my mum told me he had been in a car accident.

This smartass behaviour did not go down too well with those on the receiving end of my truths, so naturally, I went into protection mode, shut down and fell spiritually asleep for years.

> **awake (v.)**
> 'cease to sleep, come out of sleep,' a merger of two Middle English verbs: *awaken*, from Old English *awæcnan* (earlier *onwæcnan*; strong, past tense *awoc*, past participle *awacen*) 'to awake, **arise, originate**'.

Like most people who connect and communicate with Spirit, I have always felt different, like I didn't fit in. When I later found out that I was in fact, not alone in feeling this way, it brought me such comfort. The challenge was to find kindred spirits who could help me understand why I had felt this way for so long and what the purpose of it all was.

I discovered *The Celestine Prophecies* by James Redfield in my twenties. Looking back now, it was the start of my spiritual journey. Redfield talks about each individual soul being part of a larger soul group, which shares the mission of helping the evolution of the cosmos. At times, a soul from a given group incarnates itself, choosing the conditions of its life according to its needs, while the other souls observe.

This process is also known as Soul Realignment, which means that we pick our human parents and life circumstances based on our individual lesson plan for a particular upcoming lifetime. This may feel a little out there, I know, and a big ask for many people to accept as it not only means you have to take responsibility for all the shit that's happening to you, you have to let go of the victim mentality and kiss goodbye to blame culture.

Despite the profound nature of this whole process, it really resonated with me, and the more I explored the idea in relation to my own life, the more I could connect my experiences with character traits in my parents. For example, feeling as if I never fitted in as a child correlated with a memory of my parents deciding to dress me in a polo neck and kilt at primary school. Lovely, smart and very Scottish but NOT the actual school uniform, which was a blue skirt and white shirt. In their defence, it was a bitterly cold winter. However, none of the other kids wore polo necks and kilts to keep warm so needless to say I stuck out like a sore thumb. I have no idea what they said to the headmaster in defence of their decision. Still, their personalities created an experience in my life that aligned with my predetermined lesson of not fitting in.

This sticking out continued at my own hand as well as Universal intervention. When we moved town, I started a new primary school and for some reason decided to cut off all my long hair. Who would do that as the new kid in school? None of the other girls had short hair, and as many women will agree, our hair can be a security blanket. It did physically feel like a blanket had been removed. Long curly hair is heavy on your head and keeps you warm. I don't remember it being cut off (I've likely blocked it from my memory ☺), but I do remember feeling seen and exposed and cold. There was no wall of curls to hide behind. What possessed me to remove that blanket at a time when I was already vulnerable and exposed as the new girl in class, I have no idea, but the new short hair-do made me feel unattractive and like a boy. This had nothing to do with gender identity; I thought I looked like a boy, which felt alien to me as I felt like a girl. It didn't help that adults occasionally used to call me 'son' when I was out with my parents. As a consequence, I refused to go into the class, choosing to sit in the changing room until the headmistress eventually found me.

At secondary school, when my curly hair had thankfully grown back, I was bullied for being posh. Some kids will come up with any excuse to ostracise you. I was just well-spoken and well mannered. Anyway, pedantics aside, there was an advert on the TV at the time for Cadbury's Double Decker. Thanks to my big hair, the ring leaders in my year decided I looked like one of the characters in the advert. Looking back, it was rather inventive, and I'd appreciate the humour now. However, at the time, I didn't appreciate being singled out for ridicule. It was agreed by the bullies that everyone in my class was only allowed to address me (i.e. insult, spit, ignore, push and shove) as 'Double Decker'. When this was no longer considered entertaining, I was called Chewbacca from Star Wars, again thanks to my big hair. They would attempt Chewbacca's angry, forlorn, excited cry-roar that resembled a cross between a walrus, camel and lion whenever I came into class.

The bullying, coupled with the fact that my maths teacher taught us how to play poker in class while drinking vodka and Irn Bru (a famous Scottish fizzy drink), resulted in my parents agreeing that our education was a priority, so they moved us to a private (fee-paying) school. The unfortunate downside of that move was that I was then bullied for not being posh enough. You couldn't make it up. In addition to being called Chewbacca (they came up with that nickname too) and Valderrama, after the Brazilian footballer, I was on the receiving end of a lot of cruel bullying that left me sobbing most evenings for the remainder of my school years. This was not a pleasant time in my life, and to this day, I hate bullying of any kind. My heart goes out to every kid going through a similar experience, especially with the cruel addition of social media.

What I didn't realise until I had become SuccesSoul, was that this was me (my soul), via the Universe, my parents and my peers, teaching me (the human) to celebrate and embrace being an individual, special and unique in every way. My soul was teaching me the skills and knowledge I needed to speak up and use my voice to activate and rock the world. I was shown that being an outsider gave me a voice. To use that voice wisely, I needed to learn determination, resilience, self-reliance, independence, courage, compassion, empathy and forgiveness. These lessons needed to be firmly embedded in my being before I could fully activate the gifts that I was here to share with the world.

The signs from our souls are littered throughout our life, and the more we sleepwalk through it, the longer we take to reconnect with our truth. Waking up to the fact that we are here with a soul purpose, mission, path, or whatever resonates with you, helps activate your highest potential. Being awake to the idea of Spiritual Awakening is something you can choose to do. The simple act of choosing to be awake shifts the energies within you and that is enough to bring you closer to your soul path.

Chapter 5

Be a Snowflake

Accepting that you are an individual, different from everyone else, can be difficult, but necessary for your SuccesSoul journey.

When I was young, my dad told me that every snowflake that fell from the sky was different. This was mind-boggling and sent my synapses into overdrive. My instant reaction was to say, 'that's rubbish', as my young brain couldn't grasp the magnitude of such a statement so made the snap decision that it could not possibly be true. After further consideration, it wasn't long before I had fully bought into the idea, and it blew my mind. I loved the idea that every flake of snow was unique, and when they landed on trees or the street or the countryside, they collectively transformed the world into something magical. Individually their shape, pattern and design are specific to them, none more beautiful than the other. Alone they are vulnerable and can melt in seconds, but together they shape the landscape and create such beauty.

Snowflakes are beautiful, and I loved the fact that it was possible to be beautiful and different at the same time – something I did not believe as a young girl who was bullied at school. How many times have we all longed to be different, to stand out, to be special? By contrast, how long have we all tried to fit in? Like most lessons in life, they are a paradox, a contradiction. As always, the Universe loves a contradiction!

This conversation with my dad took place on a chairlift heading up a ski slope in Wengen in the Swiss Alps. It had been snowing for a couple of days, and everything was covered in a deep blanket of white crystals. It looked magical. Large flakes danced on the air as they fell slowly from the sky, and I remember tilting my head back, sticking my tongue out and catching them in my mouth. They melted the instant they were captured, flowing through the tiny bumps on my tongue into my cheeks, like fairy glen glacier melt flowing into the valley. I told you I had a fertile imagination as a kid.

There are, I know now, two types of snowflakes in this life. The six-sided hexagonal crystals that are shaped in high clouds and fall to the sky magically transforming everything they touch, and the term used to categorise young people who are offended by what they don't agree with or deem to be politically incorrect.

For the left-brain readers, here's the science bit. No two snowflakes (I'm talking about the ones that fall from the sky now) are identical. They may look similar to the naked eye, but they will be different on a molecular level due to the precise number of water molecules, the spin of electrons, isotope abundance of hydrogen and oxygen etc.

The science is interesting, but what captured my imagination as a young girl catching snowflakes on her tongue was the concept of individuality and the power of the collective. Let me explain...

Snowflakes falling from the sky completely transform everything they land on, assuming they don't melt. Snow not only changes the way the landscape looks, but it also changes the way it sounds because everything becomes quieter (snow absorbs noise). Snow makes our world look magical and beautiful (I know this is a personal opinion, but I'm sure I share it with enough readers to make it true enough to write). It shimmers and glistens, slips and crunches under our feet. However, like every fairy tale, snow has a dark side. It can be utterly destructive, engulfing everything in its path if it avalanches down the side of a mountain, and when compressed into ice to form glaciers, it can carve through solid rock.

This was what blew my mind more than anything. How could something so magical, delicate and vulnerable be so destructive? Individually, snowflakes are powerless in their ability to create any lasting impression on the world around us other than in our mind and heart. Collectively, they have the power to transform or destroy everything in their path. I'm sure the snowflakes (and I'm talking about the modern use now) relish the power they hold as a collective, even by the fact they have been noticed enough to be given a word.

The concept of being delicate and dangerous appealed to me as a young girl who felt ostracised for being different. As it turned out, it was possible to be different and be part of a powerful, beautiful, transformative collective at the same time. I would have loved to have been called a snowflake in my youth.

Chapter 6

The Truth State

Truth. A word that should have one simple singular meaning but has become individualised, different and played around with, just like the definition of snowflake. Crystal clear in its intention, undisputed and understood in every language across the world, and unchanged by time, society, history or culture. Yet it remains utterly personal and completely flexible in its definition. Why is that? How can one word have so many definitions and infinite meanings? It has caused wars, torn families apart, ended marriages, and because we lose connection with our own truth, it has caused a dramatic rise in the number of people experiencing mental health issues.

truth (n.)
Old English *triewð* (West Saxon), *treowð* (Mercian) 'faith, faithfulness, fidelity, loyalty; veracity, quality of being true; pledge, **covenant**,' from Germanic abstract noun **treuwitho*, from Proto-Germanic *treuwaz* 'having or characterized by good faith'.

When I heard the Chinese proverb 'there are three truths, my truth, your truth and *the* truth' I was a teenager, and it irritated me. Why? Because, rather naively, I believed there was only one truth, *the* truth. Something either happened, or it didn't; you either behaved badly or you didn't, you either said something hurtful, or you didn't. When this revelation first hit me, I was young, going through puberty and arguing with my siblings. My mum would sit us down and ask us to explain what had happened. The conversation would usually go like this: my brother or sister would state their case, I would state mine, and invariably everyone's version of events differed. The disagreement over the facts of whatever altercation had arisen would, more often than not, surpass the frustration I felt over the original squabble.

As far as I was concerned, everyone's explanation of the disagreement should have been the same, i.e. the same as mine. This was not an early indication of narcissism; it was a genuine, honest belief that my version of events was the only version of events. I believed that my interpretation of what took place was factually correct. In my mind, there was no 'he said, she said'. It was a specific moment in time that had only one beginning, one middle and one end. There was no room for interpretation or artistic licence. The cause of the argument or disagreement was by now irrelevant. It was the contradicting explanations of what happened that took me by surprise, and quite frankly, pissed me off.

The ensuing screaming match would usually end up with us calling each other liars, as we held our corner and defended our beliefs. I would typically end up shouting the loudest in an attempt to be heard, which was more often than not taken as a sign of aggression and I would, therefore, seem guilty of doing whatever it was we had started arguing over in the first place. My parents would understandably be exacerbated by our unhinged exchange, so the 'winner' was usually the one whose story came across most convincingly and calmly.

As I grew up, I realised there were many truths. We all have faith in our own interpretation of the facts or events that are filtered through our life experiences and our emotional responses to it. We have faith in our own truth. When we lose faith in this, we lose connection to self.

Here is the truth as I know it to be.

Most people, at some point in their lives, have been so far removed from who they truly are that they have felt lost, alone or both. Lost in themselves, in their relationships and in their work. Alone in a crowded room, on the train and in a marriage. They are not alone because they are not surrounded by people; they are alone because they have become separated from their soul. They have lost the connection to their truth. This happens gradually and subtly as we grow up and move through our life. We are seduced and stimulated by the world around us – in our defence we are Spirit having a human experience and that means immersing ourselves in the real world around us – but that does not mean we have to abandon one in favour of the other. This can be a symbiotic relationship, but like any relationship worth its salt, we need to work at it. And like every good relationship, it has the potential to turn sour if we neglect either party or favour one over the other.

The truth is we are multi-dimensional beings – mind, body and soul – and that connection needs to be embraced, nurtured and maintained for us to thrive in life. Too many of us spend too much time in our mind and body and not enough time with our soul, hence the resulting feeling of separation, loss and loneliness. When we unify with soul, we encompass our truth and therefore cannot possibly feel alone because we are connected to everyone, everything, all that is and all that will be.

Why do so many of us not recognise this truth? What are we putting off? What are we afraid of?

Chapter 7

Procrastination

In 1742, Edward Young wrote in *The Complaint: or, Night-Thoughts on Life, Death, & Immortality*, 'Procrastination is the thief of time.' This is as relevant today as it was in the 18th century.

We have all put off doing things until the last minute for one reason or another, but to chronically, knowingly avoid doing something and deliberately finding distractions to help with that avoidance is not healthy. Procrastination stems from a struggle with self-control and an inability to know how we are going to feel in the future. It is all about trust. We procrastinate because we don't believe we have the ability to create the outcome we desire, and we don't want to be responsible for doing something that might not make us feel the way we hoped.

Procrastination is such a loaded word and intricately perplexing. For many, it is a daily struggle, and for most, it results in some form of guilt, anxiety or stress, yet we all do it knowing we are going to suffer in some way for doing it. It's a conundrum – in an attempt to avoid the unpleasant, we end up feeling unpleasant.

So many of us delay the things we don't want to do, postponing what we know is in our best interests. It's an infuriating, irritating and bloody annoying habit. Have you ever watched the petrol light go on in your car but driven another twenty-five miles before filling the tank? How about leaving the dishes piled up in the sink even though you hate a messy kitchen? Jumped in the shower ten minutes before your husband is home at 6 pm? Left yourself twenty-five minutes to get somewhere even though you know it takes thirty-five? Is your daily exercise routine running for the train every morning? Ever stretched out the last of the milk with water to make a latte in the morning? Maybe said you'd book a table for dinner but by the time you got around to it the only available slots are 5.30 pm or 10 pm?

Procrastination never really goes away and can creep up on us when we least expect it. It has nothing to do with desire, motivation for, or commitment to, a project or task. However, with social media, TV, gaming etc., there are a myriad of distractions to help us on our procrastination journey.

Every single one of us procrastinates in some way or another, even the high achieving, go-getting, entrepreneurial spirits who appear to succeed at everything they do. The souls working twenty-hour days, delegating, creating and manifesting the life of their dreams, still procrastinate. The multitasking mums, juggling work, the school run and marital bliss. The professional athlete whose life is dedicated to being number one still procrastinates. Procrastination does not discriminate, and none of us are immune. We are all in this together. So, what does procrastination mean, and more importantly, what does it mean to you?

While the Cambridge Dictionary gives us a simple definition of procrastination – *to keep delaying something that must be done, often because it is unpleasant or boring* – this does not tell us the whole story because we don't all find the same tasks unpleasant or boring.

> **procrastination (n.)**
> 1540s, from Middle French *procrastination* and directly from Latin *procrastinationem*, meaning 'putting off to a future time,' 'putting off from day to day', it comes from the noun of action from past-participle stem of *procrastinare* 'put off till tomorrow, **defer, delay**,' from pro 'forward'.

Despite these informative and elegant definitions, to really understand procrastination, we have to understand why we, as individuals, procrastinate.

I'm sure, like me, many of you will have had the internal monologue about being lazy, lacking willpower, being undisciplined or thinking you've got loads of time. Anyway, the task in question isn't that important in the grand scheme of things. What are we putting off? What are we trying to control? What do we want to avoid? Why are we even asking these questions in the first place?

According to *Psychology Today**, procrastinators are made, not born. It is learnt indirectly from our family environment. For example, controlling parent/s prevent children from developing the ability to regulate themselves, from understanding their own intentions and how to act on them. Procrastination can also be a form of rebellion under such parental circumstances.

There are, according to psychologists, several different types of procrastinators. These include:

- The Perfectionist – pays way too much attention to the minutiae.
- The Dreamer – enjoys planning more than doing.
- The Avoider – doesn't do something in case they make a mistake.
- The Crisis Maker – deliberately leaves doing things until the last minute.
- The Busy Procrastinator – bit of a fusspot and has trouble prioritising.
- The Imposter – afraid of being exposed as unqualified or inferior.

Truth be told, it doesn't matter what your reason for procrastinating is, it can have serious implications on your health, time, experiences and relationships. It's something we all need to get to grips with, if we want to live a fulfilling and balanced life.

One of the biggest factors contributing to procrastination is the feeling that we have to be motivated or inspired to work on a task. The key to this is the word *feeling*. Our feelings are an emotional state or reaction. Feeling that we need to be motivated before we are happy to do something is telling ourselves that we need to be connected to our emotional self. This is when we start to understand what procrastination is.

Procrastination ultimately stems from a struggle with self and an inability to know how we are going to feel in the future and whether we will be up for doing something now or later. We are trying to assess which timeframe will give us the best/most enjoyable feeling, and we have to believe that we will make the right choice between doing it now, or doing it later based on the desire feeling outcome.

> 'I'm going to clean the bathroom now because I'll feel good about myself, and I love getting ready in a fresh bathroom.'

> OR

> 'I'm gonna clean the bathroom later. I'm tired, and I don't want to miss the final episode of [insert favourite TV show].'

Procrastination is ultimately about self-belief. And this is where the second part of the equation comes in. Trust. It's about making a choice and about trusting that choice.

> **Self-belief + trust = being proactive** (I knew my maths higher would come in handy one day!)

But like all good maths equations, there is more to this than meets the eye.

Self-belief is the way you feel about your skills, abilities, appearance and behaviour. If it has eluded you over the years, it can take time to build back up. I say back up because you were born with self-belief. Life can sometimes knock it out of us but more on that later.

Trust is the firm belief (or knowing) that something or someone is safe or reliable. It does not require facts or proof; it requires faith and vulnerability. It's about handing it over and relinquishing control (sounds bloody scary, right?). How can letting go of control make you feel more in control? This is one of the reasons why the act of procrastination is a contradiction in itself. You need to let go to find your 'get-go'.

The reality is that some of the most important truths in life are contradictory, and as you know, the Universe loves a contradiction.

- Less is more.
- The more we fail, the closer we are to succeeding.
- The more connected we are, the more isolated we feel.
- The more choices we have, the less satisfied we are.
- The best way to meet someone else is not to need to be with someone else.
- The only constant is change.

Self-belief and trust are irrevocably intertwined, a symbiotic relationship that blossoms and shrivels our desire to procrastinate. For relationships to flourish, there are sometimes unforeseen variables. The other variable in the procrastination equation is time: how we spend it, use it, feel about it and control it .

When we procrastinate, we are also trying to manipulate time so that we spend more time in a better feeling state. So, you could say that the mathematical formula to stop procrastinating is:

Self-belief + trust ^ time

I'm sure the mathematicians amongst you will have something to say about this, but you get my drift. The way to stop procrastinating is less structured than a mathematical equation. It is more fluid and organic, more intuitive. It's about connecting to your inner being, your soul self, to first understand the root cause, or the source of, your need to procrastinate. You need to look past the story about being lazy or that you will be better at something when you are more prepared. It's about moving past the doubt, around the fear and through the negative chatter to the heart of the matter – you. It's about being honest and truthful and non-judgmental. It's about allowing yourself to be you, right here, right now and knowing that is enough, and you are exactly how, who and where you are supposed to be. This does sound scary – I know, I have been there – but I can promise you that it is your ego telling you it's scary. It's creating a false sense of dread (very few people love the unknown) to prevent you from connecting with your soul self. If you do that the ego loses control, and we all know how much we hate to lose control.

If this process seems too challenging for you right now, working on your self-belief will help. Some people are born with unwavering self-belief, some are not. It is as much nature as it is nurture, and for most of us, it's a journey rather than a destination. Self-belief can be a fluid experience, with more or less of it throughout our lives, depending on where we are at personally and professionally. The great news is that there are so many ways to develop your self-belief, and as a result boost your confidence, which will, in turn, help you to learn to trust, and when you multiply that by the power of time, well, procrastination gets kicked into touch.

If stopping procrastinating is not enough of an incentive to help build your self-belief, then the health benefits should convince you:

- Better overall health because you can deal with stress and difficult emotions more easily.
- More time for your family and friends because you're able to comfortably set healthy boundaries and leave work at the office.
- Better relationships thanks to healthy boundary-setting and ability to focus on improving relationships.
- Improved performance at work through better ability to concentrate and greater commitment to tasks.
- Your energy and motivation increase, and you reduce negative thought patterns.

So where do you start? For me, it began with limiting beliefs and the realisation that self-doubt is the biggest passion killer for self-belief. It sounds like this:

I do/don't
I can't
I should/shouldn't
I am/am not

Others are/will

Sound familiar? Sometimes, depending on where we are on our journey, we can feel overwhelmed, and the thought of making any changes can be too much for us. It doesn't need to be. Some of you will feel inspired and be desperate to jump in head-first, as it's been a long time coming and you finally feel ready. For others, it's a much more tentative journey. Try not to judge and don't wish to be something you are not. You have chosen your lessons, and this may very well be one of them. Embrace who you are and reframe your outlook; welcome the learning that comes when you start to unfold and understand and accept who you are.

The internet is awash with great advice on how to increase your self-belief. Depending on your personality, different tips and exercises will work for different people. It's about trial and error (and a little patience) and finding which methods work best for you – and, most importantly, make you feel inspired to keep going.

Here are some of the things I did to help me boost my self-belief, which in turn helped me to trust. You don't need to do them all or all at once. Remember it's a journey, not a destination.

Things you can do to boost your self-belief:

> Accept a compliment.
>
> Accept a gift.
>
> List your strengths.

List the things you love about yourself and your life.

List five things you are grateful for today. Make this a daily practise – gratitude is a superpower for SuccesSoul living.

What are you proud of?

The thing that makes you unique/special is?

You are most happy when?

What is your best feature is?

How would your friends/family describe you?

Recognise the negative words you use and how often you use them. In time, you can learn to change them for more positive alternatives or remove them altogether.

Do something that pushes you out your comfort zone – like going to the public swimming pool in a bikini rather than a cossie – big ask I know, and a bold move, but well worth it.

Eat healthier, exercise and drink more water (boring I know, but it works).

Limit your time on social media – a MUST.

Read more – not glossy magazines, proper books (you will also be helping writers make a living, so this can also count as paying it forward).

Pay it forward – buy someone's groceries, even if it's only a packet of gum, smile at the guy next to you on the tube/subway, pay your colleague a compliment, offer to give your mum a shoulder massage, offer to wash your neighbour's car.

Learn to accept failure – try something that you know you are going to fail at. I'm an artist so my go-to would be trying to paint an exact replica of a vase of flowers. For me, it's an INSTANT FAIL but who the hell cares?

Ask yourself how you would help someone feel better about themselves?

Learn to reward yourself for a job well done, even if it's only putting your feet up for five minutes.

Start writing – get all those shitty thoughts OUT OF YOUR BODY and close the journal/laptop when you're done.

Meditate and practise yoga – yes, it really works.

Laugh – at a joke and yourself – as much as you can.

Run down sand dunes.

Go skinny dipping.

Smash a plate, just because, (unless it was a wedding gift or family air loom). You can always buy another.

Go out of the house with no makeup on.

Make a vision board.

Create personal boundaries. Say yes, or no, for a week/month/year.

Ask for help.

Cry in front of someone you don't know.

Set achievable, realistic goals and break bigger goals into manageable 'to do' steps, then write a list and commit to ticking things off that list. If you fail, then you have done the next step.

Learn how to fail #winwin

Share a secret about yourself.

Start a hobby, something that has nothing to do with work or family. You need something that takes you away from everything else you do in life.

Grow a plant from a cutting.

Take a dog for a walk – borrow one from family/friend or one of the official websites.

What does procrastination have to do with SuccesSoul living? We procrastinate because we don't trust our ability to create the outcome we desire, and we don't want to be responsible for doing something that might not make us feel the way we hoped. The exercises above are about reconnecting you with your feelings, which in turn and time, ignites your trust (remember it's a partnership). It can be scary to step out of the familiar, even if we are desperate for change. Procrastination stems from a place of fear, and fear is a lack of belief in your soul self.

* *Psychology Today* 'Why We Procrastinate' by Hara Estroff Marano

Section 2

The Process

This is where the work begins. Section 2 is the step by step process to help listen, take responsibility, step up, let go, open up, accept and move closer to your soul.

Chapter 8

The Feeling Revealing

For many people, myself included, it's hard to know how to feel about life sometimes. When asked what I was passionate about, I could not answer. I had no idea what passion *felt* like. I knew what it meant in my head but had no idea how it felt in my body. When I realised this, it shocked and saddened me. How could I not know what passion felt like? It struck me that in suppressing the feelings that hurt me, I had suppressed so many different feelings, and as a result, switched off my ability to really feel. I had emotions; I am human, after all. However, they were not the same as feelings. What many of us do is try to replace or suppress our feelings with external stimuli like drinking, shopping and over eating. In some cases, these external replacement feelings become addictive, and we all know where addiction leads.

We need to understand the meaning of feelings (I have included a short list and definitions for reference), how to access our feelings, immerse ourselves in them, give them their power, step aside and allow them to flow, thank them, then let them go. This is the process of revealing our feelings. Just like a physical wound takes time to heal, revealing our feelings also takes time. However, with patience and understanding, you will be amazed at what arises within you. Allowing this process to happen is not easy, but the sense of release and clarity you will feel is profound. Be patient, be loving and be kind to yourself. Honour this process and give it the time and space it needs to happen naturally, at your own pace.

Feelings. Feelings. Feelings. Such a loaded word that can fill us with dread or elation in equal measure. A word that has the propensity to render the most eloquent illiterate, confuse the most agile of brains and have most of us running for the hills in an attempt to escape them. Feelings are shunned, embraced, hidden, controlled, desired, stifled, vented and cherished. They can last for a lifetime or disappear in the blink of an eye, make or break our day and influence our decisions against our better judgment. They are the reason we can act out of character, and they have the power to hurt and heal in equal measure. They are a law unto themselves, and we spend our lives trying to live in harmony with them. Without a doubt, feelings are one of the most complicated aspects of being human.

What makes feelings such a powerful influence in our lives, why are we so eager to suppress them, and why do we need to reveal them? Before we can look at revealing, we need to understand *feeling*.

Most people use the words 'feelings', 'emotions' and even 'mood' interchangeably, but in fact, they are very different despite being close relatives.

Let's look at emotions first, as they are the instigators and the fuel to our feelings. Emotions are physical, instinctive and programmed over many years of evolution. Carried out by the limbic system, the area of our brain that deals with emotions, memory and arousal, they are hardwired, complex and involve both physical and cognitive responses.

The science bit...

> Our limbic system is separate from (sitting behind) our neocortex, the part of our brain that deals with conscious thought, reasoning and decision making. The limbic system categorises human emotional experiences as either pleasant or unpleasant mental states of mind based on our interaction with biochemical (internal) and environmental (external) influences. The limbic system is programmed to overreact (fight or flight fear response from cavemen times), which is why emotions are a knee jerk reaction based on fear and are often illogical, irrational and unreasonable.

According to the experts, there is no definitive list of emotions. However, it is generally accepted (based on which psychologist you believe) that there are up to twenty-seven basic emotions:

> admiration, adoration, aesthetic appreciation, amusement, anger, anxiety, awe, awkwardness, boredom, calmness, confusion, contempt, craving,

disappointment, disgust, empathic pain, entrancement, envy, excitement, fear, guilt, horror, interest, joy, nostalgia, pride, relief, romance, sadness, satisfaction, sexual desire, surprise, sympathy and triumph.

The good news is that you can retrain the primitive responses of your brain and not allow irrational emotions to take hold of you, which includes, very briefly: staying positive, embracing what you can't control, focusing on what really matters, letting go of perfectionism, not dwelling on problems, trusting your gut, allowing your intuition to roam freely and… having a plan b.

Now that we know what our emotions are let's look at our feelings.

Feelings are the mental associations and subsequent reactions to our emotions, and they are personal to each of us based on our own life experiences. Feelings are how we experience the world around us. They can be either physical, such as touch or pain, or they can be psychological, such as being in love. It is our feelings that determine whether we are happy or sad. They motivate us and affect the way we behave, yet they can be very difficult to put into words.

Amazingly, there are over 4,000 feelings listed in the English language. Most of us can recognise about 500, but if asked to list feeling words, we max out at about ten. This is likely one of the reasons we find it difficult to express how we feel.

Why don't you try and write a list of all the feeling words you know and see how many you get?

_____

_____

_____

_____

_____

_____

_____

_____

To recap, our emotions come first and are Universal. How we feel about these emotions is where our personal experience comes in, so the feeling associated with a particular emotion can vary greatly from person to person.

For example, you are in a café having lunch with your friends, and someone walks in with their dog. The café allows dogs, and the staff all make a fuss of the dog and give it a bowl of water. The staff clearly love dogs and feel happy about the dog being there. You and your friends may all feel differently about the dog being in a café. You may feel disgust (because dogs shouldn't be allowed where there is food), fear (because you were bitten by a dog when you were a child), curious (because even though you're not a fan of dogs, this one looks really cute) or envy (because you'd love to have a dog, but you work full time, and it wouldn't be fair on the wee thing).

Emotions are event-driven, and feelings are learned behaviours that often lie dormant until they are triggered by a certain event and its subsequent emotion. Feelings are brief and transient. Emotions, on the other hand, are felt more deeply and last longer.

Despite this newfound clarity, the distinction between emotions and feelings can still be pretty confusing. Take happiness and joy, for example. Most people think they are simply two different words used to describe the same thing. They aren't.

Happiness is a feeling based on our current circumstances. Joy is an emotion. We feel joy without consciously deciding to feel joy. Happiness is a state of mind and plays out in our heads. Joy is an emotion that is felt internally within our bodies.

Still not convinced? I love this table of examples by Sebastian Gendry on laughteronlineuniversity.com

Feelings	Emotions
Feelings tell us **how to live**.	Emotions tell us what we **like** and **dislike**.
Feelings state: There is a **right and wrong** way to be.	Emotions state: There are **good and bad** actions.

Feelings state: **Your emotions matter.**	Emotions state: **The external world matters.**
Feelings establish our **long-term attitude** toward reality.	Emotions establish our **initial attitude** toward reality.
Feelings alert us to **anticipated** dangers and prepare us for action.	Emotion alert us to **immediate** dangers and prepare us for action
Feelings ensure **long-term** survival of self (body and mind.)	Emotions ensure **immediate** survival of self (body and mind.)
Feelings are low-key but sustainable.	**Emotions are intense** but temporary.
Happiness is a feeling.	**Joy** is an emotion.
Worry is a feeling.	**Fear** is an emotion.
Contentment is a feeling.	**Enthusiasm** is an emotion.
Bitterness is a feeling.	**Anger** is an emotion.
Love is a feeling.	**Attraction** is an emotion.

Now that you know the difference between feelings and emotions (I hope), what is The Feeling Revealing and why do you need to reveal your feelings to live a SuccesSoul life?

First of all, we need to understand who we are at the most basic level. To do that we need to start by understanding our feelings, our individual responses to our emotional reactions based on our personal experiences.

Feeling Revealing Exercise

I would like you to take some time and centre yourself. Take a few deep breaths and bring your awareness into your heart centre. Can you think back to a time when you overreacted to something? This requires you to be honest. You don't need to share this with anyone; it's your secret. This overreaction can be as a child, but it's better to explore this experience as something you did as an adult. Write down briefly what happened. What was it? Where were you? Who were you with, or who was involved? How did you feel then? Write down as many words as you can about the feelings and emotions that played out at the time. Take some time to immerse yourself in the memory and see what comes up. Does this memory flood you with feelings, or is it void of emotion now?

I ask you all this because the truth is that our feelings are a culmination of the way we view our life and the people in it, so the way they feel is a product of experience or people. We are all guilty of feeling sad or pissed off and blaming it on someone else. 'If only he/she hadn't done/said that I wouldn't feel… (fill in the missing words).'

Guilty. As. Charged.

Equally, how many times have you believed that you feel happy because of something someone said or did? How many of you believe that your happiness is because of your partner, job, children, friends and family, thinking if you lost any of them, you wouldn't be happy? I appreciate that if we lost a loved one, it would have a deep and profound effect on us, but I want to express that most people believe they are happy as a result of an external stimulus.

I'm going to break something to you, so please brace yourself for a loving **#coldhardfact**

Feelings are caused by your thoughts about circumstances or people. NOT the circumstances and NOT the people.

WTF! You mean I can't blame him/her/they/it on x/y/z? Nope.

Recognising and ultimately accepting this is the first step towards revealing your feelings and taking responsibility for yourself, your reactions and your life. I know that responsibility can be a scary word for many people, but break it down as:

Response to your ability

It then becomes an empowering word full of possibility, rather than a heavy word laden with burden.

. .he second step (and the hardest) to revealing your feelings is recognising and releasing any unhealthy behavioural patterns or habits you have adopted to either mask or replace your feelings. Most of us at some time in our lives have tried to feel a certain way, or prevent ourselves feeling a certain way, by drinking, taking drugs, eating, shopping, having meaningless sex, spending money we don't have… the list goes on.

My mask was food/comfort eating and controlling what I ate. It probably started as a child when things weren't going so well for me at school. I hated the Monday to Friday school week because it invariably meant I was miserable, so I longed for the weekends. Friday night was always a bit of a thing in our house. My mum finished work for the week, and she'd bring us home some form of chocolate bar – this was back in the day when chocolate was considered a weekly treat not a daily snack/source of energy. We spent the weekend with my dad (they divorced when we were kids), which always meant a takeaway pizza and ice cream from the Italian deli on the way home. I loved those times. I felt safe and secure, so I must have connected food with parents, security and comfort, and it spiralled from there. When I lost my job on the radio, I controlled what I ate to help me cope with the feelings of rejection. I'd either not eat enough and exercise (I thought if I lost weight, I'd look better and therefore I wouldn't feel so rejected) or binge eat to mask the feeling of emptiness. Emotional hunger can't be filled with food, and it's a horrible cycle that affects so many people. I struggled to break the pattern for years because it was literally in my face every day. We cannot live without food, unlike drugs or alcohol, so the temptation for me was inescapable.

Your mask of choice and how ready you are to reveal your feelings will depend on how easy or not this process will be. Easy is subjective, I know, but the good news is that easy is possible and many people have released themselves from unhealthy behavioural patterns with time, patience and commitment. This process only truly happens when you are ready, and only you will know that when the time comes. You have to try and keep trying. Don't berate yourself for falling at the first hurdle.

I'll let you into a secret; despite having tried Neuro-Linguistic Programming (NLP), Emotional Freedom Therapy, Taping and Hypnosis to understand and explore why I had been masking my feelings, I wasn't ready until I was *ready*. When I was finally able to reveal my feelings, it was years after my first session. All these wonderful and valid modalities helped and supported me through the process, but I fell off the wagon several times over the years. At the time, I was pissed off with myself, and with some of my therapists if I am being honest, for not managing to fix or heal myself with their help. The truth is, we have to accept that true healing (The Feeling Revealing), only comes about when the route cause/s of the issue is addressed and transformed. If all we do is try to find some sort of relief, or we do something to mask our symptoms, whatever brought about the need for healing in the first-place manifests itself within the body in some form or another. Looking back, I was not fully transparent with myself or my therapists, and I wanted a quick fix. I wanted in and out, quickly. I wasn't ready to deep dive and commit to my healing, so I ended up taking longer to move through this process than I would have had I not… procrastinated.

Our bodies natural instinct is to protect itself, and it does so in the quickest most efficient way possible at the time (fight or flight), which is why, when we feel bad, we reach for the bottle, or buy another pair of shoes we don't need or take that pill. The real problem occurs when we start to rely on unhealthy behaviour to function, and it becomes an integral part of our nature.

Asking yourself what it is that you want to feel when you drink, shop, eat and engage in other vices, is the first step to releasing yourself from unhealthy behaviour. Be kind to yourself, try to lose the judgement, and release any guilt you feel. Guilt is a horrible word. We punish ourselves when we feel guilty, and that serves no one. Remember we were only trying to protect ourselves when we started this behaviour in the first place, and the likelihood is that it's gotten out of hand. We haven't recognised that we are in a different place in ourselves and no longer need this protection mechanism.

When I first started to explore The Feeling Revealing, I found it difficult. I had squashed and ignored and run away from my feelings for so long that I didn't know what feeling felt like. Does that make sense? I knew the words, and I understood them: 'I am passionate about skiing', but I couldn't connect the word passion to a sensation or a feeling in my body. How sad is that? I had disconnected from my feelings, 'accidentally' switching them off in an attempt to avoid the ones that made me feel bad.

A friend recommended *The Desire Map* by Danielle LaPorte, a book about identifying your core desired feelings and then creating the practical steps to generate those feelings. It helped me to reconnect with the feelings behind the feelings. I was struggling to verbalise my feelings and also to know what they were (which is why I suggested you write out all the feeling words you know earlier on in this chapter). Having a workbook to follow brought the structure I needed. I had to Google 'feeling words' in an attempt to find out how I felt. Try it. You'll be blown away by how many there are.

I had started to remember and reconnect with the words, which in turn started to reignite the sensations behind them. I started to feel again, slowly and, at times, painfully, but I was on the path of inspiration. My journey to living a SuccesSoul life had begun.

The truth is that we already know everything there is to know and everything we need to know; we just have to remember. Sweeping spiritual statement I know, but there you have it. Remembering who we are is about reconnecting to our soul self, and to do that we need to embrace, understand and accept our feelings. Feelings are the key to the soul. When we understand our feelings and accept who we are, we reconnect to the very essence of our being, our soul self.

The body is designed to regenerate, and just like a physical wound, reactivating our feelings takes time. Be patient, be loving and be kind to yourself. Honour this process and give it the time and space it needs to happen naturally, at your own pace. You will be amazed at what rises within you if you give yourself the freedom to explore and express without judgement. Like a disused tap of running water, once you turn your feelings back on, they will begin to flow consistently and with increasing clarity.

Chapter 9

The Clearing

Now that you have allowed your feelings to flow, your being will be flooded with realisations. Memories will surface that you have not been aware of or haven't thought about in years. You will start to feel differently towards people, places and situations. You will have clarity and confidence in the decisions you make. Rather than looking to others for the answers (this is giving your power away), you will know what to do about certain decisions or situations. This is owning your power. It may feel overwhelming at first, and like a child learning to ride a bicycle, you are likely to have a few wobbles. However, something inside anchors you with a determination to go with the flow, even if what you want does not make sense to you or those around you. This is when you start to engage with the energetic flow of the Universe. You have started to blend with your soul. At the end of this chapter, there is a step by step guide to a burning ritual that helps release and clear the energy that has surfaced as a result of your Clearing.

Once you allow your feelings to start flowing again, you do shift the energy in your body. When we hide from our feelings or lock them away, we block energy, and it needs to go somewhere. Occasionally, it might release as an outburst of some sort, or it can manifest in an ailment or illness. I know from my own experiences that I have 'manifested' health issues throughout my life as a result of blocked feelings.

In our defence, society has encouraged us to keep a lid on our emotions and feelings for centuries. It wasn't until fairly recently (in the scheme of our modern history) that talking about how we feel has been encouraged. There is a lot more to be done in this area, but I am confident we are making positive headway.

You may have heard that when your body is out of sync, it can manifest in disease, or to be more precise:

dis - ease

Pain and dis-ease are our body's way of getting our attention. According to many spiritual practitioners, including the wonderful Louise Hay, illness is an indication of your emotional health caused by your thoughts. If this is a new concept, it can be a little too out there for some. However, I suggest you read her list of symptoms and the correlation between dis-eases and the symptoms you may have experienced in the past, or are having now, and the probable causes. I guarantee if you are honest with yourself, you will relate and recognise the connection. She also provides wonderful healing affirmations to help you shift the energy surround the ailment/dis-ease.

Anyway, back to clearing that trapped energy. When I began to let the energy flow and allowed my feelings to surface, I was flooded with lost memories. Out of the blue, an image would appear in my mind, and I'd watch the memory unfold in my mind. I don't know if something triggered these memories, or if it was my body/soul recognising their significance, or the fact that I was ready to experience them again – but come they did. Some good, some not so good, some hurtful and some so full of joy I was brought to tears – I did allude to the fact that this process came with a healthy health warning ☺.

These resurfacing memories flooded my being with feeling, which is exactly what is supposed to happen. Slowly at first, and over time, with more spontaneous regularity. Far from sending me over an emotional cliff, giving my memories and their feelings free reign took the sting out of them. They lost their power to overwhelm, and this helped my confidence – in myself and in my ability to tackle previously difficult situations. It was a perpetual cycle; the more I gave space to my memories and their feelings, the more the energy shifted and released.

I found myself feeling lighter and happier. I started to chat with strangers and actively tried to engage in conversation with them – previously, I had looked down and walked past hoping I was invisible. I enjoyed the sunshine, just because it was a sunny day. I became aware of how negative my chat was, in my head and in general, and began to alter my vocabulary to include more positive words and stop the rest of a negative sentence from coming out. Problems became challenges. I spoke to myself in a softer and kinder way. I began to practise gratitude and being thankful for what I had rather than resentful for what I didn't. I kept myself busy so that I didn't have too much time to think. My relationships improved, and my energy increased.

None of this is new I know, and people have been preaching this for years, but it isn't until it happens to you that it makes any sense or holds any sway. The kickback from all of this is that in releasing the energy, you gain more energy. In letting go of the power of your emotions, you empower yourself. The Universe loves a contradiction as you know, so this should come as no surprise.

You may find that you become more sensitive to negative energy and can cope with it in a much more balanced way. I stopped watching the news. I checked the headlines, so I knew what was going on, but I stopped listening to it on the radio and watching the evening news on TV. It is so full of negativity and propaganda which is not good for you full stop. I found I couldn't watch anything violent on the TV or watch a soap/drama where all they do is argue – you know the ones? I couldn't be bothered with any drama and shied away from confrontation. I just wanted to live in my happy bubble.

Now clearly, this change can have an impact on your friends and family, and some of them may not know what to make of it. You *may* have a tendency to be a little self-righteous when you are going through this transition, and that *may* irritate your loved ones and colleagues. However, know that it is just your ego digging its heels in. Be brave and tell it to piss off! Your loved ones will thank you for it later on ☺. If they don't support your renewed self, then perhaps it means stepping away from some relationships until the energy rebalances. Many people I've spoken to about this transitional period have said they've had a 'clear out' – house, cupboards and friends.

As hard as that may feel, you will have no choice in the matter because you will know when someone is truly happy and supports your highest good. Once you start on your spiritual path, you cannot get off despite all the ups and downs – and ups and downs there are, believe me. Being SuccesSoul takes work. It takes commitment, kindness and patience. It is different for everyone, and we all have our own timeline, but somewhere deep down inside you know you have to do it. Now that you are in the flow with the Universe, you are living its contradictions. The good news is that this will not have the same impact it might once have had. It feels right despite all the new sensations and experiences, and this is because you are reconnecting with your soul self.

You can support this transition with rituals. A ritual is simply a practise that helps us focus, deal with anxiety, or feel more confident. They can increase our performance by turning small, everyday acts into more significant ones which adds more meaning and joy to our lives.

> **ritual (adj.)**
> 1560s, from Middle French *ritual* or directly from Latin *ritualis* 'relating to (religious) rites,' from *ritus* 'religious observance or ceremony, **custom**, usage,'

As you know, everybody is different, and some of you may need a little extra help clearing and releasing old trapped energy. That's ok. As there is a connection between personality type and learning style, I believe the same principle applies to our mind, body, soul connection and ritual practice. What works for one may not resonate for another. The good news is that rituals are, at their heart, purposeful intention. If doing something empowers you, ritualise it. The Universe listens to the intention behind the ritual rather than the ritual itself.

There are many different types of rituals, and the internet is full of them. Have fun exploring to see what feels right for you. It doesn't have to be complicated. Simply lighting a candle and blowing it out, letting the wind carry away a feather, or repeating a special phrase several times will suffice. Rituals are a meaningful ceremonial tool to manifest your desires, helping to release and clear blocked and unwanted energy. They help frame your intention and focus your energy more intensely.

I chose to do a burning ritual because that's what felt right for me. I have a practical and logical aspect to my personality, and I'm also very visual. I loved the idea of watching the energy being released, transformed from a piece of paper to smoke and ash. Maybe I also liked the idea of playing with fire. It made me feel like I was a phoenix rising from the ashes.

Before you read the following release/invocation burning ritual, please know that there is no wrong way to do this. You have to trust your gut and go with what feels right for you, even if your altar doesn't look like the beautiful photos on Instagram. I don't need to remind you that Instagram is not real.

Step 1: Create your sacred space or altar.
Given you are doing a burning ritual, it might be an idea to do this outside to ensure you have enough ventilation. Candles are always a great starting point, preferably non-scented or a delicate scent as you don't want it to overpower and distract you. I had collected various feathers, stones, crystals, leaves, pinecones and flower petals on walks with our dog Lucy, so I included them in my sacred space. You can use anything that you are drawn to that means something to you, like photographs or jewellery, but I feel that objects found in nature help charge the energy. I also used a cast iron decorative wok to put the burning paper in, and I did this outside.

Step 2: Intention setting and grounding.
This is by far the most important part of the ritual. You must be grounded and clear in your intention for the ritual. If you're just home from work, feeling under the weather, or had road rage with someone on the commute home, take some deep breaths, go for a walk or meditate to clear your mind and release the unwanted energy from the day. If you can't let it go, then I would suggest you do the ritual another day when you are ready.

To ground yourself, sit or firmly plant your feet on the ground outside next to your altar. Take a few slow deep breaths in through your nose and out through your mouth, enough to make you feel relaxed. Envisage a cord coming from the soles of your feet on every exhale, or on your sit bones if you're seated, expanding downwards into the ground reaching towards the centre of the earth. When the cord reaches the centre of the earth, imagine it wrapping around a golden ball of light. You are now firmly anchored and connected with Mother Earth. Now on every inhale, envisage life force energy making its way up the cord towards the soles of your feet. Feel the energy entering the soles of your feet – you may feel a tingle, if you don't that's ok, you just need to set the intention for the energy to move up through the soles of your feet and into your sacrum.

Once you feel grounded and focused, it's time to write down all the things you want to clear and release. You can start with the feelings, circumstances or people that no longer serve your highest good. You can either make a list, *Things to Release*, and put bullet points below, or you can write a letter to the Universe if that feels right, write a poem, or simply write a word or a name on separate pieces of paper. I chose to write a different feeling, situation and person on separate pieces of paper so that I could focus on letting each one go. Try to be as open, honest and sincere as you can. Once you have written everything down, it's time to set the intention. This can be as simple as 'I release everything and everyone that no longer serves my highest good' or 'I am ready to release the past and step fully into the present', or you can simply trust your intuition and roll with what comes up.

'I choose to move with grace into the life I was born to live.'

Or insert your own guided intention.

Step 3: Burning and releasing.
Once you have finished listing everything and you have
your piece/pieces of paper, it's time to burn them all.
This goes without saying, but please be careful, as you
are playing with fire. Take another few deep breaths to
settle into the ritual, and just before you ignite the paper,
say a little prayer – this does not need to be a religious
affair. I use prayer in the loosest sense of the word.

Dear Universe,

*Thank you for supporting me on my journey and for
helping me with this releasing ritual. I am now ready to let
go, with love, all energy that no longer serves my highest
good. I am now ready to release the feelings,
circumstances and people from my life that no longer
serve my highest good. I no longer need the lessons that
these circumstances taught me, and if I have not already, I
vow to learn the lessons in a different way that opens my
heart and frees my soul. I ask for Mother Earth's help in
transforming any negative energy back into love.*

If you work with angels, then you can include them when
you ask for help.

As you light the paper and watch it burn, say, 'I release
you with love.' You can also rub your hands together
effectively 'washing' yourself of any attachment to what
you have released.

Continue to do this until all the pieces of paper have
been burnt, and you are left with a pile of ash. I like to
pour the ash onto the ground. I found a lovely spot in the

woods, but your garden is just as good, or the beach, wherever feels right for you. I then stood on the ash and stamped and smudged it into the ground. As I did this, I asked Mother Earth to accept my offering with love and asked her once again to turn any remaining energy that no longer served me into love.

The key to a burning ritual is release. You have to truly want to release and let go of everything you have included in your ritual. When you truly let go of your expectations, the Universe is free to provide for you abundantly and creatively. There is also no wrong time to do the ritual, go with your gut, but new moons and full moons are always a more powerful and potent time for energy work. The moon has a powerful influence on us as spiritual beings, as it is the closest astronomical body to us. The full moon offers the most profound energies that we can absorb, while the new moon is the next most powerful energy. Working with the moon's energy can guide us to find the inherent wisdom and truth within ourselves.

The full moon marks the completion of the (waxing) cycle and the growth cycle of our intention. The full moon's energy is at its peak and is very powerful, so you can use this energy to see what is no longer serving your intentions.

The new moon energy will help create fertile ground for your seed to grow, so take time to nourish and heal your body, mind and soul. As this time is about new beginnings, allow yourself the opportunity to put thought into the intentions, dreams and goals for your future.

It is common to feel overly-emotional and disconnected at the peak of the full moon phase, but use its energy to help understand what is no longer serving you, then work with the new moon energy to help support new beginnings through your releasing ritual.

A note about clearing rituals and your expectations.

Sometimes when you release unwanted energy, you find yourself on a high. You have cleared what you wanted to shift, and you move forward feeling lighter and more inspired. However, this is not always the case. Releasing blocked energy can sometimes open the flood gates, so don't be surprised if you feel emotional for a few days and a whole load of stuff comes up. If this does happen, try to remain calm, breathe into the frustrations and don't react. I know this can be easier said than done, but forewarned is forearmed, and everything that is happening around you is for you, by you. Allow the energy that surrounds this phase to flow whichever way it needs to. You can support this phase by practising self-love/self-care in whatever shape that is for you – even if it's simply taking a bath or a few moments to yourself. Ask those around you to support you with whatever you need. If those around you are embroiled in the ragged energy, take time away from them or let them know that anything said or done during this time may not be how you truly feel. This phase will highlight cracks in a relationship as well as cement them. Remember, you have to be willing to let go and TRUST the Universe. If you do, you will ride the bumps with grace.

Chapter 10

The Quickening

After The Clearing, you have The Quickening. When a blocked artery is cleared, the blood courses through your body, refreshing and re-energising every cell. The Quickening is the energetic equivalent of this process. Your being will be flooded with fresh new source/Universal energy from the initial rush of letting go of old and trapped energy. You will feel alive, vital, inspired and powerful.

Part of being SuccesSoul is letting go of old patterns, and sometimes that means there will be casualties. Despite feeling empowered to step into the new you, there will be a knowing that this detachment has consequences that may affect those most dear to you. It is human nature to want to run before we can walk. However, we have to be able to fully understand our new-found power, and that takes time and patience.

When this chapter title came to me (as much of the book did) intuitively, I had a chuckle to myself. The Quickening is the perfect description for this stage in the process of SuccesSoul living for a number of reasons. These days, time seems to be speeding up. Hours, days, seasons and years fly past. Biologically speaking, quickening is the process of showing signs of life. In pregnancy, first foetal movements are called quickening (often described as flutters by expectant mothers).

Despite the relevance of the meaning above, it was actually a film reference that I connected with, and if any movie fans are reading this book, the term may be familiar to you too. The Quickening is a phenomenon in the *Highlander* films and TV series, and rather serendipitously, it was the film's 30th anniversary in 2018 which was the year I came up with the title of this chapter, so it seems meant to be.

The first time I watched *Highlander*, I was a teenager in the late 1980s, and Christopher Lambert was Conor McLeod, an immortal swordsman born in Scotland in the 16th century. McLeod was *very* attractive, mysterious and slightly damaged, which turned out to be a lethal and potent combination for a pubescent girl. Suffice to say, the character and the story left a lasting impression on me. I still love this movie and must have watched it a dozen times.

Anyway, back to the film plot. Beheading a character known as an 'Immortal' produced a powerful energy release from their body called a Quickening. The lead cast member of the television series, Adrian Paul, said: 'The Quickening is the receiving of all the power and knowledge another immortal has obtained throughout his/her life. It is like the receiving of a sacrament or a massive orgasm.'

While there are no beheadings on the journey to SuccesSoul living (orgasms, however, are most definitely a side effect of SuccesSoul living), there is a shift away from the ego-mind. Given that the mind resides in your head, the beheading analogy isn't too far off the beaten track. I'm being a little flippant I know, but The Quickening in SuccesSoul living is the process of receiving or reconnecting to source energy and knowledge. It is empowering, it makes you feel alive and vital and quite frankly, immortal.

On the subject of power and knowledge, Francis Bacon, an English philosopher, statesman, scientist, jurist, orator and essayist famously wrote 'knowledge is power' in his book *Meditationes Sacrae*. First published in 1597, it is regarded as one of the most important religious writings and was an attempt to mediate the reformed English church between the two extremes of Popish superstition and profane superstition.

What has this little factoid got to do with The Quickening? Three things.

1. It's important to know where something comes from, hence the little fact about Francis Bacon because we are the culmination of our history, ancestrally and socially.
2. It's important to keep learning something new (assuming you did not already know this – I didn't).

3. It is an important reminder that knowledge is more powerful than physical strength, and no great work can be done without knowledge.

Knowledge is what you will gain from your SuccesSoul journey, and the more knowledge you have going into this journey, the more empowered you will be. I believe, having been through The Clearing and The Quickening, that had I known then what I know now, I would have had an easier transition, and I wonder if I may have accomplished more. One could argue I had the experience I was meant to, but there is nothing wrong with imparting a little wisdom in the hope that it is of benefit to others on their journey.

This was my experience. I hope you find it useful.

The Quickening was a gradual process for me over a few weeks, but it was noticeable. I was aware there were subtle but dramatic changes taking place in me, and as a result, around me.

From the initial rush of letting go of old blocked energy – like me, you supported and supercharged this process with the burning ritual if you did one – you will start to feel more alive, vital, inspired and powerful. You sense within your being that a shift has taken place. Something has lifted, and you feel lighter. As this energy continues to circulate through you, it builds momentum and starts to affect how you interact with the world around you.

Naturally, I was buzzing about this transformation. It felt like it had been a long time coming, and my cup was overflowing. My husband noticed that I was behaving differently. I was outwardly happier and generally on better form. My sense of humour came back, and I didn't take everything to heart – previously I'd been sensitive, and if someone was taking the piss (how the Scots compliment or show affection), I would react rather than enjoy the banter.

> **banter (v.)**
> 'attack with **good-humoured jokes** and jests,' 1670s, origin uncertain; said by Swift to be a word from London street slang. Related: *Bantered*; *bantering*. The noun, 'good-humoured ridicule,' is from the 1680s.

This was a wonderful feeling, but like everything in life, there needs to be a balance. We can have too much of a good thing and feelings are no exception. It's all too easy to jump on The Clearing juggernaut and hurtle headfirst into the future, oblivious of everything and everyone around you. It is normal to be seduced by these feelings. However, we have to remember that our newfound self may be vibrating at a different level to our nearest and dearest, and they may take time to understand and accept the new you.

Remember, The Clearing is like the first rush of love, or the rush you get from the first draw on a cigarette when you haven't smoked in a while. It is quick, all-consuming, euphoric even. But like every good high, it can give you a false sense of wellbeing because it provides an escape into your imagination. And once your mind starts to work its magic, well, you're on a slippery slope if you let it run wild.

I don't say any of this to scare you; I say it to *aware* you. A good guide is sensitive to your needs, organised so they have everything covered, and knowledgeable so you have all the facts.

Chapter 11

The Flashbang

This is the kickback to The Quickening and is part of the process of finding soulful equilibrium. Out of nowhere, you may experience flashes of extreme emotion. This will come as a shock to you and may feel like hitting a brick wall because you have been on top of the world after The Quickening. This is natural, healthy and necessary.

Think of it as a Spiritual sales course; the Universe is trying to sell your ego a new car (the car is symbolic of the journey you are on). Your ego wants a top of the range, all singing all dancing sports car. It wants speed and power. The Universe only has a clapped-out banger that needs care, attention, time and effort to keep the engine running. It takes forever to get to the destination, and your ego is not buying into this. To add insult to injury, the Universe wants a shit ton of money for this banger, and there is no way you can square away spending that amount of money on a rubbish car. You have to realise that change takes time and comes with a price. The banger will get you there and teach you a lot in the process. The Flashbang stage also tests whether you truly have started to trust the Universe.

We know the Universe loves a contradiction, and for every ebb, there is flow. It is an energetic exchange, and there cannot be one without the other. There has to be balance for life to grow and evolve, and humans are no different. The tricky part, as you well know, is finding that balance. Recognising you need to lead a more balanced life is the beginning of the journey, and for many, one of the hardest parts. Finding and sustaining that balance is where the real skill comes in. And I do mean skill:

> **skill (n.)**
> late 12c. 'power of discernment,' from Old
> Norse *skil* 'distinction, ability to make out,
> **discernment, adjustment**,' related to *skilja* (v.) 'to
> separate; discern, understand,'

As you know, knowledge is acquired through experience or education, by perceiving, discovering or learning. To lead a balanced life, one must perceive (or remember because you are born already knowing everything) and discover through trial and error or learn through curiosity.

The kickback to The Quickening is what I like to call The Flashbang. The Flashbang is the yin to the yang of The Quickening. It is the leveller and the equaliser. We know that too much of a good thing is not good, and that includes The Quickening. When you reach that state of being, despite loving being in it, you have to set it free.

You can choose to do this yourself, or the Universe steps in and does it for you. Enter The Flashbang.

A flashbang, if you are not familiar with the term, is a non-lethal explosive device used to temporarily disorient an enemy's senses, and while this isn't warfare, this stage in the SuccesSoul journey can feel explosive at times. When you move through The Clearing and The Quickening, you begin to step into the flow of your life. You have begun the process of shifting and releasing energy to enable transformation to take place. This is wonderful and creates moments of true joy. It also enables deeper energies to surface, and these tend to be emotions and experiences that you have suppressed for a long time, sometimes lifetimes, and you may not know they were there because they have been so well hidden.

Thanks to all the hard work you have put in clearing and releasing, you have enabled flow. And flow it does. Out of nowhere, you may experience flashes of extreme anger, tears and emotion you can't verbalise.

The Flashbang is the release of energy or emotion that has been trapped for so long it erupts out of the blue. The truth is, it's not actually out of the blue, but you will have been so distracted by all the positive energy flow that you have ignored or missed what was happening beneath the surface. I like to think of this as an erupting volcano. As a visual person, it helped me understand what was happening because The Flashbang felt physical as well as emotional.

Your trapped emotional history is like magma bubbling away deep under the surface. A volcano is an opening in the Earth's crust that allows gases, lava and ash to reach the surface and escape into the atmosphere. The Flashbang and The Quickening are like the volcano. They have created an opening which makes it possible for the release of built-up emotional energy.

Remember you did a burning ritual? You can liken the release of the smoke from this to the release of the gasses from a volcano. You created a weakness on the surface that enabled the release of pressure. The Flashbang is like the eruption of molten lava. It is shocking, spectacular, frightening and over in just a brief moment. The minute molten lava is released into the atmosphere, and it starts to cool off.

As knowledge is power, I hope knowing that you may experience little mini emotional eruptions will help you and those around you understand and release them with love. The release of this emotion is followed by doubt. As a more awakened soul, you are no longer able to ignore and squash back down challenging emotions. You are brave, you feel stronger and want to tackle them head-on. That's when the exploration takes place. You want to understand where these deep-rooted emotions have come from and what they mean. Sometimes the answers will come to you and sometimes they won't. This can lead to frustration and doubt in your belief that you are truly connecting with self and source.

It was round about this time that I started to 'square go' the Universe ☺. For the non-Scottish readers:

square go
A Scottish **call to fight**: 'When one's patience has been exhausted (i.e. you're pissed) by the aggravating assailant, the cry goes up for a 'SQUARE-GO!'

Don't worry about this ridiculous reaction. It's normal, and I promise that you will smile and laugh about it later. The fact is you are ultimately challenging yourself to a fight, and one could argue (☺) that's a good thing. It means you care about what's happening to you, and you want to move through it. That said, in my humble experience, wanting to 'square go' is your ego resisting change. You are holding on to old habits and behaviours that are years and lifetimes in the making. It's a struggle to let go and trust, and for most people, this takes time and patience and practise.

I found listening to 'letting go' meditations very helpful, having tried to learn to let go by myself. As I wasn't very good at it, I started listening to Jason Stephenson on YouTube every night before I fell asleep. It was sometimes a passion killer, but I was determined to support myself, and I found his voice very soothing. Jason Stephenson has studied the positive effects of guided meditation and relaxation music for over fifteen years, and his YouTube videos have over 250 million views (at time of writing). Russell Brand calls him a 'gentle Australian brain alchemist', and I couldn't put it any more eloquently.

If listening to mediation isn't your thing, then there are other ways to help you transition through this phase with grace. Reiki, emotional freedom therapy, past life regression, shamanic work, yoga, mindfulness, journaling, exercise, good old-fashioned patience, honesty with your friends and family, and an acceptance that sometimes you just have to be vulnerable to be brave. All this and asking the right questions. It's important to remember that the Universe listens to the energy in your questions rather than the words you use. If you find you're not receiving answers, it might be a timing issue, but it might also be that you are not phrasing your questions correctly.

I have found it frustrating at times that ripping the plaster off didn't work. I should have slowly and meticulously peeled it off gently, but my impatience invariably got the better of me. My soul knew that patience was a lesson I was here to learn. It, therefore, threw up new obstacles to slow me and my awakening down. What I should have done was place my hands over my heart, take several slow deep breaths to reconnect to my inner wisdom and ask myself, 'what do I need in this moment to support what is happening to me?' This is a great tool at any time when you feel out of whack, and the more you do this, the quicker the answers will come. It's also another great way to reconnect with your soul self, which is ultimately what you are trying to achieve.

Chapter 12

The Slump

By now, you will have begun to notice that the journey to SuccesSoul living has a few highs and lows, or more accurately, times of proactive flowing energy and times of passive retreating energy. You will also appreciate that life is about balance; there will always be toing and froing until things settle down.

The Slump is one of those retreating times, and truth be told, an unwelcome but inevitable stage in the process to SuccesSoul living. The Quickening is such a high. It's seductive, and we don't want it to stop. The Flashbang hits and you feel taken aback, but you still have some of The Quickening energy flowing through you which keeps you upbeat and able to stay strong. The Slump is when the disappointment sets in because the positive energy you were carrying with you from The Quickening has started to rebalance, and you sense your old reality/thought patterns/energy creeping in. You will begin to question things, old fears may begin to resurface, and you may feel a little dejected that the highs of The Quickening haven't lasted. Fear not, you will deal with this part of the process much easier than initially seems possible.

A little background on highs and lows…

> SuccesSoul living is about balance, not about a life of highs and lows. And when I talk about highs and lows, I am talking about the highs under the influence – of alcohol, shopping, drugs, food, in fact, any of the stimulants we use to try to feel good about ourselves, to try and fill the hole of knowing that something is missing from our lives. And the lows are the inevitable kickback from the highs.

> A life of extremes, no matter how good the highs feel, is not living to your highest potential. In a place of extreme, we are in truth, searching for meaning and purpose. Without those, our life can feel empty, like something is missing, hence filling that gap with some form of extreme behaviour. When you are in the high times, yes it feels good, but that feeling is always short-lived, and you need to push it a little more each time, so you get the fresh buzz. I don't need to tell you about the high hangovers. I'm sure you've all experienced the fallout from overspending, over-eating, drinking too much etc. When we live in a place of extreme, we are blinkered and reacting to our emotions. Remember, emotions are irrational. Life is intense and overwhelming, and our bodies are just not designed to be on alert all the time. This way of

living is not healthy, and at some stage, you either try to find balance, or it takes control of you.

Early on in my SuccesSoul journey, I was gutted to find out that I would lose the highs. I was so used to the buzz of feeling 'happy' in those moments that the thought of losing them was quite frankly terrifying. They were the moments that kept me going. I resisted the change I knew deep down I needed to make because I did not want the good times to go. My highs were my security blanket. When things weren't going so well for me, or I was feeling flat, I clung onto the memory of the good times, waiting until I was back on the giddy, fun, rollercoaster again. They were my happy place, or so I believed at the time.

When I finally succumbed and accepted (grudgingly I admit!) that I was going to have to change the way I was living if I wanted to be SuccesSoul (and I really did), I hurtled headfirst into The Slump. I did not pass go or collect the $200; I went straight to the fun jail. Perhaps this would have been a good time to slowly peel off that plaster, but no, the Universe ripped the bandage off good and proper.

I look back and smile to myself about all the madcap mayhem I used to get up to when I was in my high times. They are very fond memories. They were expressions of my character, and it makes me feel happy to know I had fun. But I don't want to be living that way anymore. I know that I can dip my toe in the water if I ever feel like it, so I haven't actually lost anything. I can tell you that fairly soon into The Slump I saw the light, and if someone could have waved a magic wand and taken me back to those high times, I would not have gone. I knew that I was doing the right thing for me. It became clear that I had quite the imagination (given all the ridiculous things I used to get up to when I was pissed!) that needed a healthier creative outlet – more on that later.

In hindsight, it wasn't as bad as I thought it was going to be, but it did take a little adjustment. I stopped partying as much, which was no bad thing, and started to take better care of myself. I found fun in other healthier ways, and you can too, whatever your high is. You may feel a little resistance to what I am saying, 'give up my nights out/shopping/smoking/drinking… eh naw!' However, deep down inside you, your soul knows you are on the right path. You can, and will, make the adjustments you need to without too much resistance. It kind of just happens – proactive flow – and whilst it may sound terrifying at that moment, it's not. You will have heard of the expression that, 'fear is always worse than reality' – well this is one of those times.

You must remember that the person you are now, having gone through the process so far, is not the same person you were at the beginning of this book. You can tackle new experiences and processes with your newfound SuccesSoul superpowers. The Slump brings up unhealthy habitual behaviour (you know the kinda things I'm talking about), talking down to yourself, pulling challenging energy to you, obstacles, resistance in general. You might sneak the odd wee fag, or prowl eBay for the next bargain. You may put your energy into a project, and it doesn't go as planned because you had a *bad feeling* about it from the start. Relationships may start to have their moments, and your patience might get tested more than usual. There are any number of different manifestations for The Slump energy, but it will likely make you feel like you have regressed a little and that's not going to sit well with you given you are on a mission to be the change you so desire.

So why has The Slump arrived, and how can you move through it with as much grace as you can muster? I told you that you're a different person now. Grace was most likely not in your problem-solving vocabulary or toolkit before this.

The Slump is another obstacle on the road to trust. Plain and simple. We carry lifetimes of experiences and it's going to take a little more graft with grace to reach your goal. I believe we are the sum of many past lifetimes, and we carry all those highs and lows with us. You don't need to believe this, but it is my experience that we all carry soul history, which may explain why you feel drawn to people and places that mean nothing to you in this lifetime.

Reincarnation aside, it does not alter the fact that The Slump is about letting go and about trusting. It's about letting go of how we respond and react to things – not about being numb – but not feeling attached emotionally to certain situations or outcomes either. It's about learning to know (or more accurately remember) that certain things don't work out because there is something better around the corner. It's about recognising that something failing was never about it succeeding, it was about what you learnt trying to succeed. It's about allowing feelings to surface and giving the energy a route out without it dragging you down with it. It's about stepping aside and letting Universal flow… *flow*. It's about connecting to Universal consciousness and knowing that you are held and safe and not alone. It's about believing that the world is not out to get you, that things aren't being sent to deliberately trip you up. It's about trust.

> **trust (n.)**
> c. 1200, 'reliance on the veracity, integrity, or other virtues of someone or something; religious faith,' from Old Norse *traust* ' help, confidence, **protection, support**,' from Proto-Germanic abstract noun **traustam* (source also of Old Frisian *trast*, Dutch *troost* 'comfort, consolation,'

It's easy to trust the Universe when you are going through The Quickening and life is flowing beautifully. However, trust is only really trust when life is not going the way you want it to. That's real true trust. It's the moment when you're on your knees, the shit has hit the fan, and you step gracefully forward in a state of pure and utter acceptance. You have handed it over, and in doing so you are rewarded with a sensation of knowing that everything will work out, you are held, and so it is.

> 'I am safe, I am held, everything is as it's meant to be, everything will work out as it is supposed to. I am safe and so it is.'

The first time I experienced true trust was when my husband and I bought our first house together. We had been renting and decided to sell both our properties and buy our dream home. We are both homebodies, so a property is more than a roof over our heads. It's our sanctuary and an extension of who we are as people and a couple. For those not familiar with the property market in Scotland, the seller pays for a survey – it's called a Home Report – that lets any prospective buyers know the condition and value of the property. Each area of the house is graded on its condition. Grade 1 means good condition that does not need any immediate attention, and our home was given this grade in nearly all categories.

But not long after we moved in, I started to remove the old wallpaper from the back bedroom. When I pulled off a long strip of paper (very satisfying), I noticed a damp patch on the wall. As I worked through the house, I found damp patches everywhere. The chimneys in four rooms had been blocked up without ventilation and the roof (which had been given a Grade 1) was leaking and rotten. The front room downstairs and the back kitchen had rising damp. None of this was picked up in the Home Report. What started off as a redecoration project, very quickly turned into a money pit that resulted in a new roof and a complete internal rebuild.

We decided it was time to move out when we woke up one night with water pouring onto our bed from the roof. We had managed to squeeze our king size bed into the single front bedroom – it was the only room that didn't have damp all over the walls – so we were looking forward to sleeping in a musty free room. It was an average Scottish spring evening; the wind was blowing a hooley (Scottish for strong wind or gale), and it was raining diagonally, bouncing off the roof. We joked (yes, we still had a sense of humour at this stage in the proceedings) that we hoped the slates managed to stay on the roof before falling asleep. I remember floating in that transient space between dreams and reality hearing a *drip, splash, drip, splash, drip, splash*. I'm not sure how long this went on for, but at some stage, it morphed into a 3D dream when I felt something small, wet and cold land on my face every time I heard *splash*. I'm not a heavy sleeper (a kick-back from the insomnia of previous years), but I do have pretty vivid dreams, so it took a little longer than it should have for me to realise what was happening. By the time we both woke up, fumbled across the mattress to locate the light switch on the wall next to the door (it was a new house, we were sleep-deprived and disorientated), we laid eyes on our new indoor water feature which was missing Neptune, his chariot and several thousand coins!

This was just the first list of issues we faced with the property. There were many more with the rebuild, but I imagine you get the picture. The project cost us five times our original budget. We cashed in our savings, borrowed money from family and saved everything we earned to get the house liveable.

Those who know me, know I hate injustice of any kind. How could the surveyors get away with not doing their job properly? We decided we were not going to let them get away with it and hired a solicitor after the parent company of the surveyors told us they would not reimburse us for the money we had spent to bring it to the grades we originally bought it for. Whether we won our case or not was irrelevant by this point – in my mind they needed to pay for what they had done.

We had bought the house with a view to it being our forever home, where we might one day raise a family, so there was a lot riding on it. In addition to all the problems with the house, we had our third miscarriage. Given my age and my fertility issues, I knew when we fell pregnant there was a high probability of us losing the pregnancy. Despite 'preparing' ourselves for this outcome, we naturally still hoped for the best, so it was no less devastating when it happened. I was literally and proverbially on my knees, and that was when it happened. Trust.

I remember sobbing my heart out one night asking the Universe why all this was happening. I was at the end of my tether and couldn't see a way out. I said aloud through my tears, 'I'm out, it's over to you.' I meant every single word. At that moment, I felt utter relief. It was instant, and it took me by surprise. That was swiftly followed by utter belief. I knew without a shadow of a doubt that it would all work out. Despite everyone telling me to the contrary, I felt calm in the knowledge that the Universe would look after us. I trusted and handed it over.

I am not suggesting that you need to find yourself on your knees before trust flows. My story is just an example of what handing it over was like for me.

Trust is tricky when things aren't going according to your plan, and some of us have trust issues that we are here to learn how to overcome, through our relationships – to others and with ourselves. The Slump is a process that assists our learning. Part of the challenge is your ego being tested. It will always want to control things. You are not going to be able to detach yourself from a lifetime worth of lessons in a short space of time. However, you can live with those lessons and learnings without judgement. The Slump is about learning to coexist, without attachment, with unwanted feelings, and these unwanted feelings are the energetic footprint of your soul's journey on earth. You will not be able to rid yourself of them, but you will learn, through the process of trust, to accept that your soul self-did the best it could in each and every situation across the ages to assist your ascension.

Chapter 13

The Seeking

Where you will be at the end of The Seeking:

- You will feel more confident with the process of trust.

- You will notice your thoughts more and check the negative ones.

- You will have started to feel rather than think positive thoughts and wishes.

- You will begin to detach from old emotional baggage, and there is less connection to each *issue*.

- You will know in your soul that there is a new path for you; a new way of being, living, feeling and working, but you can't quite visualise it yet.

I loved this stage of my journey to SuccesSoul living. It was a subtle but deep shift in my transformation. Looking back, it felt like the first stages of freedom. Freedom from my past and from attachment to the future. In fact, it was likely that this was the first time I was really being present. Whatever it was, it felt liberating. There was a sense of calm and hopefulness at the same time.

The journey so far is likely to have a few bumps, and you kind of accept that because you are committed to the transformation. When you do ease into The Seeking, it feels hygge.

> **hygge (n)**
> a quality of cosiness and comfortable conviviality that engenders a feeling of **contentment or wellbeing** (regarded as a defining characteristic of Danish culture).

The reason it feels hygge is because you are much more connected with feeling. You have embraced your feelings, and the energy is moving much more freely now. Half the battle with our feelings is not the feeling itself, it's the thought about the feeling. When you feel more than you think, it feels, well, easier.

This shift and the realisation that you are stronger than you thought has helped you build your confidence - in yourself, in the Universe and in the process. You have begun to trust and let go - just baby steps - but the results have given you the proof you needed to shake off some of the fear and negativity that you felt around this whole awakening process. This confidence has a lot to do with your new sense of freedom, and that has come about because you have been practising the art of trust and learning that it is the door to your soul.

So, how do you go about trusting so that The Seeking becomes a new way of life for you?

As you have seen in each stage so far, trusting is an integral part of the process. The first step is the desire to want to change. This is something you feel you have to do. This desire arrives as a lesson, or a sequence of lessons, depending on how quickly we recognise the lesson. Sometimes our lessons are wrapped up in soft fluffy blankets; sometimes they are delivered by an arrow. Whichever way your lessons come is a pre-agreed contract with your soul and will likely vary throughout your life. Divorce, illness, loss, bullying, eating disorders, addiction, friends that let you down, stress – these are all lessons, but they don't start off as the 'end result' that finally makes us pay attention.

For most of us, we only pay close attention when our lessons are delivered by the arrow and have an impact so great that it stops us in our tracks. This can be a difficult pill to swallow because we all want the fluffy blanket option and often with hindsight, we see the warning signals clearly. When you feel that something is not quite right, instead of ignoring it or talking yourself out of it, listen.

> **listen (v.)**
> Old English *hlysnan* (Northumbrian *lysna*) 'to listen, hear; **attend to**, obey'

Explore why you feel the way you do. Do not allow your ego to steamroll over the feeling and convince you that you're being silly or that it must be your hormones or stress. Give the feeling the freedom it deserves, allow it to surface, and explore what it wants to tell you. Once you do that, the answers will come.

Giving your feelings the freedom to flow can feel a little scary. However, allowing them to do so is part of learning to trust. It's about knowing (trusting) that you will be safe no matter what. It's about knowing that you may feel out of control, but that's ok. I am not a psychologist, and I can only share my own story, but I do know from my own experience that fear, vulnerability and trust are all closely linked and are the blocks that prevented me from being SuccesSoul. If allowing your feelings to surface and trusting the Universe that you will be all right feels too daunting, you can start by learning to trust yourself.

These simple everyday exercises are small steps you can take to start to build confidence in yourself (and the Universe) rather than trying to tackle big life-changing situations before you are ready. Remember baby steps lead to giant strides.

Daily Trust Exercises

First things first, have some *me time*, and I mean spend time on your own in solitude. No people, no phones, no computers to distract you. Just you on your own. You can do this at home or on a walk, sit on a park bench and just be.

Talk to yourself, ask yourself how you are feeling, what's going on with you and see what comes up. You simply ask yourself, 'what is going on with me at the moment?', 'how am I feeling right now?', 'what is missing from my life today?' and wait to see what surfaces. Don't be put off if nothing comes up when you first try this. Be patient and be ok with not knowing at that moment. You can either ask yourself internally or ask yourself out loud. It's important to give yourself some space for the answers to surface. I suggest doing this after you have centred yourself and have some time and space. Honour what comes up for you, and don't berate yourself for it – even if it's anger. Try to explore the feelings that surface – writing is a great way to assist the flow of feelings. It enables a higher level of engagement and therefore more focus.

Make a list of the things you love about yourself. I would suggest writing them down, as we pay more attention this way. Stick them up so you see them every day.

Do something out of your comfort zone – and start small. Have that tricky conversation with a colleague/friend/family member. Take charge of your monthly spending – look at your bank account. Say no to that new top on eBay even though it's only £3, eat something unusual for the first time, smile at everyone you come across, do all your food shopping for an entire week, watch a really old black and white movie – even better if it's a silent movie – go to the cinema alone, dine alone in a restaurant, start online dating, say NO for once in your life. When you do something out of your comfort zone, it sparks your curiosity and inspires self-belief. The good news is we can train ourselves and learn to have more self-belief. It just takes commitment.

Eat, practise, sleep, repeat!

Trusting is accepting that you've got to step out of your comfort zone, knowing there are no guarantees that you won't feel hurt or let down. It's about losing the fear of the unknown, which can be a challenge as our lives have been set up to support our fear. The good news is that you can lose that fear because you were not born with it. You developed it over your life as a result of society, your upbringing, your peers and the choices you made. Our natural state is not one of fear; it is of love, and you can return to that with time and a little effort. By this stage in the process of SuccesSoul living, moving away from a place of fear is non-negotiable. You know in your soul that you have to do this because you will never feel joy if you have fear.

Vulnerability is one of your greatest strengths in releasing fear and embracing trust. To be vulnerable is to be in a state of trust. It took me a long time to be vulnerable, and I'm still working on it, but it has a tremendous power to bring you the best that life has to offer. If you don't put yourself out there, you miss out on so much. Remember you are a soul who has chosen to have a human existence – what a waste of a trip if you didn't do everything you could to experience all you could.

You should, I hope, be in the habit of sharing how you are feeling with yourself. Sharing how you feel with family or friends is a great way to 'feel the fear and do it anyway'. Fear is all about being vulnerable. Once you see that friends and family don't judge or react the way you thought they might, this builds your confidence. When we open ourselves up and talk about our feelings, thoughts and fears, we release the energy that is wrapped in the words.

By now, you are learning to trust yourself because if you don't trust yourself, how can you trust the Universe? It's about learning to trust your judgement and your ability to make good choices. It's also about not beating yourself up if you make a poor choice or you end up failing at something. Failing is part of life, and we fail our way to SuccesSoul living.

This is not an exercise. It should be part of your daily SuccesSoul practise:

- Start by looking at all the good choices you have made in your life, all the things that have and are going well for you. This can be your friends, health, career, finances etc.

- Make a list of the times when the outcome was positive when you listened to, and acted upon, your instincts. Look at this list and experience the feeling of trust.

Look over this list on a regular basis to remind yourself you are able to trust. Doing this will help you trust smaller situations that still irritate you and mess up your day. As an example:

My energy seems to interfere with tech energy, whether it's emails, phones, remote controls or computers. One time I could not send or receive emails for a couple of weeks. As I work for myself, I have no colleagues or IT support to help me when this happens. I was unable to send client documents and could only contact them using my mobile. As the days turned into a week, I became increasingly irritated until I eventually lost my shit when a folder of archived emails disappeared. Despite being on the phone most days to my email provider, we could not get to the bottom of the problem.

I'd been so wrapped up in my frustration that I forgot all about trust. My mum reminded me to practise what I preached; that letting go, handing it over and trusting would resolve the situation. That evening I sat with the energy that was bubbling away inside me, really feeling into it. I wanted to understand why this was happening and what the lesson was. By this stage in the SuccesSoul process, you will recognise that life is trying to teach you something when things appear to 'go wrong'.

> Sometimes we can get in the way of ourselves and cannot see the wood for the trees. A great way to bring through clarity when you are overwhelmed with emotion is to align or rebalance your energy (you can do this sitting or lying down). Take a few slow deep breaths to help centre yourself and feel into your heart space, then place your right hand over your heart and your left hand just above your belly button. The right hand gives energy, and the left receives energy. The right hand sends Universal loving energy from your heart, and the left hand receives Universal loving energy. You are sending love from you to you. This simple energy rebalancing acts like a natural sedative. It calms and soothes you back to a sense of harmony and clarity.

After sitting with and rebalancing my energy, I knew that I was being reminded to trust. I was trying to control a situation and in doing so, blocked Universal flow. I went to bed that night feeling calmer than I had in days. When I woke up the next day, I received a call from one of the tech guys at my email providers, and he fixed the problem in minutes.

The next time something happens to you, instead of getting worked up if you can't fix it, rebalance your energy using the exercise above. If you miss the bus, don't get pissed off, trust another one will be along in a minute, and there was a reason you weren't meant to get that bus – even if it makes you late. If someone cancels a meeting, don't call them for everything because you made time to see them, trust you'll catch up another time. If someone you fancy doesn't swipe right, trust they were not meant for you at this time.

Learning to forgive is also the key to trusting, and it starts with forgiving yourself.

forgive (v.)
Old English *forgiefan* '**give**, grant, allow; remit (a debt), pardon (an offense),'

We have all said and done things we wished we hadn't and regretted it immediately afterwards. We may still be doing something that isn't healthy and living with daily guilt at not stopping the destructive behaviour. This is the case for many people who have become addicted to something. There is no time for regret or guilt; you did what you thought was right at the time, even if you knew you were making a mistake. Our bodies do their best to protect us, and sometimes that protection can be misplaced and damaging to our health and others. Remember, we respond emotionally, and we know that energy isn't necessarily coming from a place of balance.

This is why it's so important to forgive yourself for any wrongs you think you have done – to others and to yourself. If you can't stop beating yourself up for poor choices, you will not be able to move on because you will drown in guilt and regret. Get these two words out of your life, pronto!

Knowing that things are meant to be, and will work out, gives you an inner calm and confidence. You are held and exactly where you are supposed to be. You no longer react to situations the same way you used to; you are more chilled out, relaxed, going with the flow. You also know that this is not the end of your journey, and that there is more to learn. But you are ok with that and ready to move forward in the process. You have one toe firmly in the water now, but you also have one toe out. You are cautiously optimistic, open and ready for what's to come. You feel hope and have faith that life is supporting you. It feels like a release.

The Seeking is still about implementing the trust lessons, but you are not afraid to try and don't get knocked in the way you used to when things perhaps don't work out the way you thought they might. You are taking more risks with your feelings, and your confidence is building. It feels good.

Chapter 14

The Calming

Such a beautiful space after the topsy-turvy episodes of the journey so far. The Calming is all about:

- Relaxing, trusting and letting go.
- Knowing and acceptance.
- Feeling lighter.
- No longer searching for a quick fix.
- Realising that nothing is personal. It happens for you not to you.
- Not needing another person's approval.
- Having more energy and sleeping more soundly.

Aligning with the ways of the Universe once again, The Calming is very much a contradiction. At this stage in my SuccesSoul transformation, I realised that I didn't have to keep racing ahead to get ahead. By taking my foot off the gas, putting the gears in neutral and allowing my life to unfold under its own steam, I found out that the path that lay ahead of me was full of opportunities. The same ones that I had previously, desperately, tried to make happen – and a few unexpected ones thrown in for good measure.

Before we explore The Calming in more detail, I want to share with you the definition and history of the word calm. But first, I'd like you to sit for a moment with the word **calm** in your mind. Explore what happens when you put your full attention on the word. What do you think about the word? Do you feel it in your body? If so, where can you feel it in your body? There are no right or wrong answers to this; it's simply a fun way to reconnect with yourself and an interesting experiment. Once you read the origin of calm, sit with this new meaning and let it flood your being. What comes up this time, does it feel different?

> **calm (adj.)**
> late 14c, **of the sea**, 'windless, **without motion or agitation**;' of a wind, 'light, gentle,' perhaps via Old French *calme* 'tranquillity, quiet,' or directly from Old Italian *calma* 'quiet, fair weather,'

The original meaning of the word calm – that is 'of the sea, without agitation' – really expresses what The Calming is all about. It is a shift in our emotions, which as you know can be volatile and unreasonable, to a place that is much more tranquil.

The sea and water have always been associated with humans, and we have been forever fascinated, enchanted and inspired by it. Life cannot survive without water, but it is more than that. We are in awe of the sheer scale of the oceans that separates us from other people and cultures. We are drawn to the possibility it holds, the life it contains, the adventure it inspires and the healing it provides.

Water has been used as an analogy for our emotions since ancient times when we understood that our emotional body was like a body of water – you may have heard the expression 'opening the floodgates' and 'going with the flow' as descriptions of how to manage our emotional states. Water does not try to control; it flows through the path of least resistance. It adapts to the environment, and the environment is modified by it. It is pure lifeforce energy, and as our bodies are 70% water, it is no wonder we are so inexplicably tied to it.

Thousands have lived without love, not one without water. W. H. Auden

Now let's break this down a little more and consider the word agitation:

agitation (n.)
1560s, 'debate, discussion' (on the notion of 'a **mental tossing to and fro**'), from French *agitation*, from Latin *agitationem* (nominative *agitatio*) 'motion, agitation,' noun of action from past-participle stem of *agitare* 'move to and fro,' frequentative of *agere* 'to set in motion, drive forward; keep in movement'.

The notion of a mental tossing to and fro, like a debate or discussion, is exactly what has been happening within us prior to arriving at The Calming. Our minds have been awash with debate and discussion, of contradiction and making deals with ourselves, a higher power and others. We have been all over the place, pulled from pillar to post in a state of indecision and confusion, which has left us mentally exhausted and physically drained.

The Calming is when this all stops, or at the very least slows down to a pace that does not drench us on a daily basis. The constant action of doing and being recedes. This stage does not require you to actually do anything. It just happens as part of the natural process of SuccesSoul living, and it creeps up on you without warning, which is a wonderful surprise.

Let's be honest here. For most of us, life is a rollercoaster, and so far, the process of soul reconnection hasn't proved to be much different. Sometimes, people want to bail before they reach The Calming, which is a shame because it is such an amazing stage of this process. It not only arrives without warning for those who are committed to the path; it seeps into your pores and is in full swing before you notice it. It's pure spiritual stealth mode!

The first time I realised I was in The Calming was when I noticed that life seemed to flow for me. Opportunities arrived without me having to 'strive' for them, which was the most obvious sign of The Calming, or being in a state of flow.

We were living in Glasgow at the time, and we had been dealing with a lot – the house renovation, health issues off the back of it and future decisions about what direction we wanted our lives to go. We decided to book a trip to Bali. I had always wanted to go, having drooled over the photos on Instagram, and I needed a change of scenery and culture. I've always loved travelling and exploring different countries. The smell that hits you when you first step off a plane is both evocative and intoxicating. It echoes past adventures and inspires memories yet to be made. Whether it's the crisp fresh blast of cold air in the alps, the sweet blanket of frangipani at a holiday villa, the spicy aromas of a sprawling bazaar, or the heady fishy mix of sea salt and two stroke engine oil at the harbour. I love the taste of smells, and I come alive when I can indulge my senses in an exotic paradise. I longed for adventure, and I felt I needed to reconnect with myself. The previous year had been emotionally and physically draining.

When we arrived at the airport, high winds had delayed our incoming flight. After several hours delay, we were told that we would miss our connecting flight to Amsterdam, so they wouldn't let us on the plane. There were more than three hundred passengers all kicking off, and my husband was getting stressed that our perfect holiday had not started as he had planned. If I am being truthful with myself, and with you, I would have been stressed out too, but for some reason I was calm. I mean genuinely calm, not pretend calm or suppressing my frustration calm. This struck me as odd, but I embraced it.

The airline staff were trying to add passengers to different flights over the next few hours to move the backlog. We hung in there, hoping we would manage to catch a flight and salvage the start of our trip. We were next in the queue to be rerouted when I overheard the couple behind us who were going on their honeymoon. The woman was upset, as you can imagine. I decided we should give them our place in the queue, and they ended up being the last passengers put on a flight to Dubai. We missed the cut off so had to spend the night in Glasgow before flying out the next day. Rather than being pissed off, I felt good that we had salvaged the start of that couple's honeymoon.

Meanwhile, the remaining passengers were being tricky and unpleasant with the staff at the check-in desks who had been working flat out trying to reroute everyone. I overheard one passenger service agent say she had not been to the loo for six hours and had stayed on past her ten-hour shift to help everyone with their onward journey. I decided to buy her some water and chocolates (for energy). Who was this person I had morphed into? When we finally got to speak to her nearly seven hours into the delay, I handed the gifts over. Her face softened, and her energy shifted. We had a moment of understanding, of connection, of compassion.

She explained that the next available flight wasn't until the following afternoon from Edinburgh. We thanked her for her help, and she thanked us for the water and chocolates, telling us to wait until she confirmed our rebooking.

We sat with some of the other passengers who were pretty annoyed by this point, most of whom had been put up in two and three star hotels on the outskirts of the airport. Given we lived in Glasgow, it would not have been unreasonable of our passenger service agent to ask us to head home for the night with our new tickets for the flight the following day. But something in me felt we were in for a surprise. I can't explain it, but I knew we would not be going home. When she called us over, this wonderful woman explained that she had organised for a taxi to take us to Edinburgh that night, and she had booked us into a five-star hotel including dinner, bed and breakfast. It just so happened Edinburgh was super busy, and the only available rooms were suites. Talk about good fortune.

Looking back, I know this was SuccesSoul living in full flow. Throughout that whole experience, I trusted that everything would work out, and despite all the obstacles we were faced with, we would not leave the airport disappointed. I have to tell you that my husband had no idea who he married that night. I was different from my old self, and he was a little freaked out.

You may remember in Chapter 11, I talked about The Flashbang and The Quickening being like a volcano erupting? The week we arrived in Bali, Mount Agung, a volcano on the island, had threated to erupt for the first time in more than fifty years. Following a series of hundreds of mini earthquakes, the volcano started to spew steam and smoke. Nearly fifty thousand people were evacuated from their homes; many had to leave their livestock, airlines cancelled flights and two thousand passengers were stranded. Thankfully, despite the mountain being in view of our resort, we were well out of the exclusion zone. The whole thing really affected me, not because I was concerned about whether or not our flight would be cancelled, but because the locals had been moved to evacuation camps that were overrun and understocked with supplies. I wanted to stay and do something to help.

This holiday had been a turning point for me, and it wasn't the turning point I had planned when we originally booked it. I was hell-bent on going despite my husband and friends suggesting something cheaper and closer to home. Something within me was aware that I needed to be on that island.

While we were there, we visited Pura Tirta Empul not far from Ubud. For Balinese Hindus, the spring water from the Tirta Empul Temple is holy water said to have been created by the God Indra and believed to bring sanctity, serenity and luck. The Temple was built in 926AD to honour Vishnu, the Hindu god of water, and local Balinese Hindus have come for over a millennium to cleanse their minds, bodies and souls in the curative waters of the pools. To this day, visitors can join locals and participate in the purification ritual by bathing in the holy water. I was ready for divine guidance, and I immersed myself fully in the whole process.

We hired a guide to learn the history and symbology of the rituals, which involved moving through three different pools with a number of water fountains in each. As this was a sacred site, we had to cover our swimsuit in a sarong, which we did with dozens of other tourists from every corner of the world, all laughing and giggling in a large communal changing room. Our guide explained that we should start the ritual with an offering – known as *canang sari* – which you see all over the island. Visually beautiful with delicately woven leaves, colourful fragrant flower petals and burning incense, they are mini works of art. Each piece in the offering has a deliberate and meaningful placement, selected for what they symbolise or which Hindu god they represent. For example, white lime for Shiva, red betel nut for Vishnu, green Gambier for Brahma. A small offering of coins or food is often placed on top of the arrangement, and each *canang sari* is unique and based on the feelings or needs of the creator.

We took our offerings to the edge of the first pool and were guided to sit for a moment and allow the burning incense to carry our prayers or intentions skyward towards the gods. I have no idea how long I knelt by the pool visualising my hopes for the future floating towards fruition, but I felt a connection to my surroundings and energised by possibility. The holy springs bubble into a large crystal-clear pool and gush through thirty different waterspouts into the sacred purification pools. The first pool focuses on cleansing your spirit and soul, the second on karma and getting rid of bad actions you've done, and the third pool cleanses the body of illness and also cleanses the soul. We arrived early in the day to avoid the inevitable throng of tourists, which meant the breeze in the trees and hypnotic gurgling water drowned out most of the chatter. The water was pleasantly cool in the first pool as we stood in a short queue, immersed to waist height, waiting to take our turn. The air around the top half of my body was moist as the spray from the water mixed with the humidity, incense and the jubilant tourists. When I arrived at the first waterspout, I followed each bather before me by dipping my head in the water, splashing my forehead with it, then washing it over the top of my head while in prayer or deep thought. I repeated this three times before scooping some water into my hands, putting it in my mouth, then spitting it out.

When we were initially told to do this, I was concerned about the thousands of other mouths that had spat out the water. Our guide assured us the water from the spouts was filtered, despite it tasting like it came from a fish tank. Truth be told, I felt a tad silly for even considering the sanitary ramifications of such a ritual given it had been safely practised by millions of people. *Trust* unsurprisingly popped into my head! Committed to activating my future and letting go of the past, I allowed the water to permeate my soul, flowing with each step as it took the path of least resistance towards my life purpose. I lost all sense of time and place, only momentarily aware of the hollow echo inside my skull each time I inhaled to escape the water shrouding my head and face. It was a unique spiritual experience that has stayed with me to this day.

It is true that all water is life-giving, and our love of water is pervasive. It is no surprise that in almost all cases when we think of water – or hear water, or see water, or get in water, even taste and smell water – we feel something. It is only now that I have been through this process that I recognise what was happening on that day in Bali. I was in The Calming.

This was my experience of The Calming, and yours will be very different. Like me, you may not realise what is happening until you are in it, or out the other side. The first thing you notice is that you do feel different. There is a lightness to your energy that feels permanent rather than fleeting and surface. I must point out here that you don't change as a person. You won't become unrecognisable, and you won't start doing things that are so far out of character. You will be you but on a good day!

The Calming is about releasing expectations of yourself and of others. The outcome becomes less important to you, and you don't get affected if the outcome is different than you may have anticipated. You accept that not everything will work out the way you want, and you are not hurt, disappointed or angry that they don't. You know in your soul that something better (more aligned) is out there for you and you welcome that into your life.

The other noticeable difference is that you stop looking for the one thing that is going to 'fix you' because you know you are not broken in the first place. You will likely find that balance and moderation replace yoyo and extremes. You can go out and have a glass or two of wine rather than the bottle followed by three cocktails and chips and cheese on the way home. You don't need to keep trying new diets or slamming yourself at the gym in an attempt to shift a few pounds. You know you are more than your belly or thighs, and you feel grateful and blessed that your body works. You don't hit the online shops when you can't find something to wear; you look at your wardrobe of clothes and rekindle your love of something old because you remember how you felt the first time you wore it, and you know you can immerse yourself in that energy the minute you put it on. You may also realise you have far too many clothes and end up taking them to the charity shop. This stage is about excess and the realisation that excess of any kind is not balanced. You will find that instead of it being a hardship, balance is a welcome release.

On the good days, you will feel like you are floating through life without much effort, and on the not so good days (you are human, after all, and we have external influences that can knock us at times), you are less likely to respond irrationally. You don't have the same frustration or anger in you, so other people's negative energy bounces off you more easily. You stop taking things personally – I remember reading somewhere that other people's opinion of you is none of your business – I never fully appreciated this until The Calming. You feel confident, not in a cocky way but in a graceful way that inspires and attracts people to you. You will feel generous of yourself, time and energy. You get more out of giving than receiving, and you want to share what you have learnt to activate and inspire others on their journey.

I also enjoyed my own company more and moved from occasionally feeling FOMO (despite my age and intelligence, yes I still got FOMO on occasion, I'm only human after all) to embracing JOMO. I enjoyed taking our dog Lucy for a walk and heading to a café alone. I could people watch and not feel rude for not talking to my companion. On that note, whether you own a dog or not, you will feel a pull to spend more time in and with nature, whether that's simply buying house plants (or not killing the ones you have), creating a window box herb garden, heading to the local park to read and chill, walking on the beach or hiking in the mountains. You feel the energy from nature. And it could not be The Calming without it having a positive effect on your sleep.

The one thing I feel duty bound to tell you about is that you may, *may*, move away from certain people and situations in your life that no longer serve your highest good. This can be a natural, painless transition. However, it may not be, depending on the lesson you have to learn at this point in your own transformation. What I can do is reassure you with all of me, that however this releasing unfolds, you will feel the better for it. You will know in your soul it is the right thing to do, despite any potential turmoil it may temporarily cause. You are prepared, ready and committed to moving forward with your own awakening. Release those who do not support you with love, and step into your future from a place of compassion – for yourself and the others you no longer connect with.

Chapter 15

Own Your Essence

When you Own Your Essence, you step into your power. You are an outward reflection of the inner shift back to your soul self.

> In philosophy, essence is the property or set of properties that make an entity or substance what it fundamentally is. Essence is also a condensed version of something. It is powerful, strong, and a little goes a long way.

How do you learn to Own Your Essence?

How do you share the 'new you' with the world?

Often when we are excited by something new, our enthusiasm can be overpowering. Not everyone will be ready for you as an expression of your pure essence. You may wish to learn to share it in more subtle ways with those around you who may feel uneasy about the new you. This chapter explores ways to do that.

Own Your Essence. As I write and say these words in my mind, I can feel them on the tip of my tongue. I feel inspired to explore the meaning of *essence* – the way it sounds, the way it feels as it moves through my body, the promises it holds and the knowledge I am yet to uncover.

Owning Your Essence is a deeper expansion of The Calming. It is the next 'level' in your soul full evolution. The transition, or flow, between these two stages, is therefore subtle and fluid, and you may not be aware of being in one or the other in the early stages. You might even dart from one to the other seamlessly without realising it, or you may knowingly step back and forth, to and from The Calming for a short term fix 'security blanket' if you are feeling drained or affected by life's inevitable bumps. None of the decisions are conscious. I merely mention this to make you aware and hopefully recognise yourself when you read this. You will know you Own Your Essence when you fully start owning your essence.

> A quick aside. I apologise for the riddle 'You will know you Own Your Essence when you fully start owning your essence.' I always hated when people passed on wisdom that was delivered in a bloody riddle! *Just give me the fecking answer and stop being so freakin smart!* Clearly, that was the old me, pre The Calming, now I know better ☺. Using ambiguity intentionally encourages us to analyse and reflect on our own understanding. The good news is I don't plan on leaving you wondering. I will explain what I mean below. You have enough on your plate to analyse and reflect upon as it is.

Owning Your Essence is when your inner (soul) transformation is expressed externally (body/physical reality).

> **'I am an outward reflection of the deep transformation back to soul.'**

Say this a few times before you read on. It's important that you fully connect with its meaning.

> **'I am an outward reflection of the deep transformation back to soul.'**

Awakening, unfolding and reconnecting with your soul self is a gradual process that develops over time. This allows you to become more aware of the shifts in your energetic being throughout the process. So many people spend the greater part of their lives consciously unaware of their soul self – certainly not fully integrating with or expressing this aspect of their being.

To experience a SuccesSoul life – that is harmony, balance, wellbeing, meaning and purpose in every aspect of our physical life here on earth – it is necessary that all aspects of our energetic being are integrated as a whole. We are then able to move freely, intuitively and with ease between each aspect of our being. The most important aspect of this integration is the one between our soul and our personality.

Our soul is our direct connection to source/God/Oneness/the Universe, and as a multi-dimensional being, our soul holds the vibrations of our true essence. Our personality is made up of the physical, etheric, emotional and mental body and is how we experience the physical world around us.

You may have come across the expression, *'You don't have a soul. You are a soul. You have a body*.'* I don't need to explain to you the difference between having and being, and the importance of the distinction between them; you can see just how different being a soul and having a soul are. I don't know about you, but I seem to remember being taught that we had a soul – this is perhaps why I relied on the separation of the two to understand my own Spiritual Awakening. I know I am a soul in a body having a human experience, and I connected with this truth fairly early into my own journey. You will connect to that truth in your own time, but knowing you are a soul rather than you have a soul creates a very important shift. You take ownership of being a soul, and you naturally embody that truth. You take responsibility for your body, as it will carry you through this trip called life.

Now that we've cleared that up let's look at Owning Your Essence which is essentially stepping back into your power. I personally don't love the word power in this context because it has too many negative overtones for my liking. I was guided to use essence instead. In fact, if you look at the meaning and history of both, you will see that essence is the right word in this instance.

essence (n.)
late 14c., *essencia* (respelled late 15c. on French model), from Latin *essentia* '**being**, essence,' abstract noun formed (to translate

Greek *ousia* 'being, essence') from *essent-*, present
participle stem of *esse* 'to be,'

power (n.)
c. 1300, 'ability; ability to act or do; strength, vigour,
might,' especially in battle; 'efficacy; **control**, mastery,
lordship, dominion; legal power or authority;
authorization; military force, an army,'

When we talk about essence in the human sense, it has
an elusive almost unattainable quality to it. When
describing someone whose essence is noticeable, we
sometimes say they have the 'X factor', or they have a
certain 'je ne sais quoi'. It is an indefinable quality that
makes something distinctive, made all the more
attractive because we understand it to be hidden from
view. Either way, it is strong and a little goes a long way.
As you know, only a few drops of vanilla essence in
baking makes a real difference to the flavour.

It is important to know how to express your essence. It
can be tricky to navigate being in your own essence
because it can initially feel overwhelming. You are
bursting with new (or remembered) soul/source energy,
and it is completely normal for you to want to spread the
love. But like all things in life, you have to learn to walk
before you can run. Put the proverbial brakes on your
newfound exuberance, enthusiasm and lust for life. Why?
Because it can be a little overwhelming for others who
may not be vibing at the same level as you yet. You may
end up spinning them in the opposite direction.

I say this not to cast a shadow over your light, but to
lovingly remind you that we are all on our own journey.

While it truly is wonderful to finally reconnect with your soul self and express your essence as fully and freely as you can, it is more loving to consider where other people are at. Balance your brightness to suit the eyes of those you wish to shine on. In short, not everyone is ready for you to go Full Spiritual on them, so you need to back the fook off – a little goes a long way, just like vanilla essence ☺.

Well, how should we embody our light without blinding the world? Easy. We draw on the energies of The Calming, and we remember to be light and gentle, if and when we need to be.

Use your awareness to find the right level of energy until you can instinctively share yourself in a compassionate, considerate and loving way. Over-excitement is an extreme emotion and a lack of self-control. Remember, emotions are carried out by the limbic system and our limbic system is programmed to overreact. We can choose to have soul control (self and soul are interchangeable) by choosing to surrender to Universal energy, our higher self, our soul. Without that conscious choice to put your soul in control, you cannot completely embody the full essence of your soul. The path to choosing soul control is to choose love. Love is the key that opens the door (our heart) to our soul. When we integrate the physical with the spiritual, we cannot help but find ourselves in a place of love. Love, by definition, is considerate and compassionate and full of empathy.

In your defence, you are in a state of high momentum; your soul self is buzzing, and your physical body may not have fully caught up – hence the exuberance. You have, as part of your SuccesSoul journey, had an influx of energy that opens your psychic centres otherwise known as your chakras (see note on chakras at the end of this chapter) and heightens them intensely. This is one of the reasons you feel buzzed and full of excitement.

I am not suggesting that you stop shining your light and embodying your essence. I am simply recommending that you use your common sense, read the situation and share your light in more subtle ways IF the situation requires it. A genuine loving smile can have more impact than an exuberant rant about how wonderful the world is and how amazing you feel. This balancing act is really your ego's attempt to regain control, and as long as you are aware of that, you will strike the right balance and the ripple effect of the 'new you' will be far-reaching.

A Note on Chakras

There are seven main chakras in the body, from the base of the spine to the crown of the head. Chakra is Sanskrit for wheel or disk. Chakras are invisible wheels of energy where matter and consciousness meet. This energy, called Prana, is a vital life force which keeps us vibrant, healthy and alive. Each chakra corresponds to nerve centres in the body as well as major organs, and our psychological, emotional and spiritual states of being. Since our chakras are energy and therefore moving, it's essential that they stay open, aligned and fluid. If there is a blockage, energy flow is restricted.

Starting at the base of the spine:

First (root) Chakra: The *Muladhara* is the chakra of stability, security and our basic needs. It encompasses the first three vertebrae, the bladder and the colon. When it is open we feel safe and fearless and is associated with the colour red.

Second (sacral) Chakra: The *Svadhisthana* chakra is our creativity and sexual centre located between the pubic bone and the navel. It is responsible for our creative expression and is associated with the colour orange.

Third (navel) Chakra: The *Manipura* chakra is the area from the navel to the breastbone and is the source of personal power, self-esteem and energy. It is related to the metabolic and digestive systems and is associated with the colour yellow.

Fourth (heart) Chakra: The *Anahata* chakra is located in the heart centre and unites the lower chakras of matter and the upper chakras of Spirit. The heart chakra serves as a bridge between our body, mind, emotions and Spirit and is our source of love and connection. It is associated with the colour green.

Fifth (throat) Chakra: The *Vishuddha* chakra is located in throat area and includes the neck, thyroid, jaw, mouth and tongue. This is our source of verbal expression and the ability to speak our highest truth. It is associated with the colour blue.

Sixth (third eye) Chakra: The *Ajna* chakra is located between the eyebrows. It is also referred to as the 'third eye' chakra and is our centre of intuition. We all have a sense of intuition, but we may not choose to listen to it. It is associated with the colour indigo.

Seventh (crown) Chakra: The *Sahasrara* chakra, or the 'thousand petal lotus' chakra, is located at the crown of the head. This is the chakra of enlightenment and spiritual connection to our higher selves, others and ultimately the divine. It is associated with the colour violet.

The exercise in Chapter 13 where you placed one hand over your heart and the other below your navel was a chakra rebalancing exercise. You placed your right hand over your *Anahata* chakra and your left hand over your *Manipura* chakra.

* 'You don't have a soul. You are a soul. You have a body.' Often incorrectly attributed to CS Lewis, this is from *Annals of a Quiet Neighborhood* by George MacDonald.

Section 3

The Payoff

This section explores the shift in energy as a result of working through the step by step process. These new energies will flood your body, mind and soul and here is where we look at what to do with it all.

Chapter 16

The Calling

Without warning, you feel as if you are going with the flow rather than against it. You feel connected energetically to the Universe. You didn't try to make this happen, it just gently rose to the surface of your being and was. The Calling is different for everyone, so this chapter helps you to recognise the signs that you are plugged into life and therefore ready to remember what your gifts are to share with the world. We all have something special to offer, and it is rooted in service of others. Service is not a sexy word, and few people want to be in service, or of service. The reality is that this is what makes us tick. Your Calling is the how-to part of getting a kick out of life. When we are aligned with our true self, our Calling is the energetic transfer of service. Nothing else can stimulate us so completely with love, and the more you give, the more you receive. Your Calling is how you share that gift of love with the world.

This last section of the SuccesSoul process is where everything comes together for you, and you remember what your purpose is. That might sound like a sweeping statement and an impossible task. When I was feeling lost before I went through this process, I would not have believed that I would discover what my purpose was despite being desperate to know it. I obsessed over what my soul purpose was, spending hours on the internet Googling the meaning of life purpose and soul purpose, trying to find someone or something that would help the penny drop. Needless to say, I never found the enlightenment I was looking for because I wanted a quick fix, and that's not how life or awakening works.

Purpose and meaning are the foundations of a happy, fulfilling life, yet they can be elusive for many of us. Most of the time, we have no awareness of them until we find ourselves in our thirties, wondering what the hell we are doing/going to do with the rest of our lives. This is normal; most people spend the first three or four decades of their life living the human experience without much awareness of their spiritual being. I must note that things are definitely changing, and many more people are coming onto their spiritual path much earlier in life than my generation and beyond did, which is a wonderful thing.

It doesn't matter at what age you reach this point in your life; the feeling is the same. You realise that your life needs more depth, more connection, more feeling and more meaning. It needs to make sense. I find it interesting the meaning of *meaning* in Hindu is breakthrough and release, which is exactly what happens when you find that elusive meaning in your life.

> **meaning (n.)**
> c. 1300, *meninge*, 'sense, that which is intended to be expressed,' also 'act of **remembering**' (a sense now obsolete), verbal noun from mean (v.). Sense of 'significance, import' is from the1680s.

Your SuccesSoul journey is about remembering. You were born with all the knowledge for this lifetime. When we search for meaning and purpose in our life, we are simply trying to remember.

While I was trying to work out what to do with my life, in my search for more meaning and purpose after I saw my papa in my living room, I took several mediumship and psychic development workshops to try and understand what I could and should do with my heightened intuitive senses. After my session with Jessica (the wonderful Swedish Wizard), she suggested I find a local reiki healer to try and shift some of the blocked energy. She said that this would help me understand what I was supposed to do with these new (or remembered) gifts/abilities. I found a lovely reiki practitioner, Lorna McLean, who confirmed my mediumship abilities after our session. We discussed whether I wanted to develop them or not and 'yes' popped into my head before I had the chance to consider it. She told me about an Australian trance medium and teacher called Jennifer Starlight. Lorna had worked with her in the past and said she might be able to help me. I booked a Skype reading with her the following week. During our reading – which I entered into with an open mind and no expectations of what I wanted out of it – she told me that I was a medium and a psychic and asked if I wanted to do something with it. She also told me that if I chose to do something with it, the journey would not be easy. Again, just like my conversation with Lorna, I said yes, and in that moment, a strange butterfly tingling sensation spread over my chest across my heart. It felt like a very subtle but obvious energy pulse, similar to when your heart skips a beat, and you can feel it in your chest and mouth. Jennifer explained that this was the energy shifting within me, and whenever I needed to find the answer to a question, I should be aware of the same sensations.

Jennifer guided me to the Arthur Findlay College and suggested I book a course with them. The college is an international residential centre where students study Spiritualist philosophy and religious practice, Spiritualist healing and awareness, spiritual and psychic unfolding and kindred disciplines. I affectionally call it Hogwarts. The same day I had my reading, I found a course, and booked my flights. This is something I would never have done before. I always considered the cost of things before I spent a chunk of change on something; even my husband was surprised by my financial spontaneity.

When I arrived at Hogwarts, I was like a duck out of water. There were nearly sixty people on the week-long course from all over the world, and many of them had been practising mediumship for years. **I. Did. Not. Belong. There.** Turns out I was wrong, but I'll get to that.

Most of us were in small dorms or shared rooms, which was weird for me having not shared a dorm since a riding holiday in the Scottish borders as a child put me off bunking for life. Despite feeling awkward, I was open to the experience and went down to the welcome meeting. During a meditation, when I had my eyes closed, it felt like my grandmother's face was right up in mine. I could feel and see her in my mind's eye as if it was real. I felt a subtle pull towards the right side of my face, like my energy was trying to move closer to her. It was strange, yet comforting, and was followed by the most overwhelming, all-encompassing and powerful sensation of pure love. It was unlike anything I had ever felt before, and if I could have stayed in that moment forever, I would have. It was then I realised I was in for a rollercoaster of a ride that week.

Three days later, I was ready to pack my bags and head home. I called my husband and sobbed like a homesick teenager. I had not managed to connect with anyone during the various classes and felt like a fool and a fraud. I felt exposed, vulnerable and completely lost. He told me to stick with it one more night, and if I still felt the same in the morning, he would pay for a flight back home. Something made me share how I was feeling with my teacher, who suggested I give the afternoon session a go. If I still felt unable to open up to Spirit, then she understood my reasons for leaving. She had that little glint in her eye; you know the one? People 'in the know' have it.

We began the afternoon session working with angel cards and tea leaves, which are used as divination tools for connecting with Spirit and exploring the past, present and future. After pairing up, and mediating with the cards (in my case staring in a blank fixated trance at the cards), the teacher asked us to share what had come through to us with our partner. It turned out the angel cards did not work for me. I drew a blank, nothing, nada. Not a name, a memory, anything that I could share with my partner other than the words and colours on the card – which was not exactly intuiting anything. Talk about awkward! I sheepishly apologised to the woman and moved on to the tea leaves in the teacup. I could feel my body recoiling in on itself with embarrassment. Everyone else appeared to be having great success at this card reading malarkey. How the hell were tea leaves going to help me 'see' when a card with words and images on it didn't? I was out of the frying pan, jumping headfirst into the fire, and I did not like it one bit.

When we paired up for a second time, I decided honesty was the best policy so apologised in advance for being crap at readings and told the man opposite me not to expect anything profound, helpful, or inspiring. I had all but switched off from the whole process. I planned to bumble through the rest of the afternoon session, call home and get that plane out of there.

> Tea leaf reading, or Tasseography, has been used by fortune tellers for centuries. They look at the patterns and shapes left in cups after drinking tea and interpret them as prophesies and messages from the past, present and future. It quickly became popular across Europe as a means of telling fortunes because all you needed were a few tea leaves.

Up until that day, I had never tried it, or known anyone who did, and given my crash and burn angel card reading, I didn't hold much hope for this. I followed the instructions about how to prepare the tea to read the leaves (if you fancy trying this I have included instructions at the end of the chapter) then stared blankly at the dark shrivelled leaves scattered randomly around the inside of the cup.

To my surprise, the more I stared at the scattered leaves the more I began to see symbols and shapes – like finding elephants and ducks in clouds. Stories emerged from the shapes and triggered my imagination. Out of nowhere, a whole load of information came out my mouth. I can't remember what I said, but the guy was nodding in agreement and smiling. He even asked me a question to see if the leaves held the answer. **I. Was. Buzzing.**

Buoyed by my little breakthrough, I was excited to see if this was more than a one-hit-wonder. Turns out it wasn't. That afternoon I did a reading for a woman who had been trying to connect unsuccessfully with her brother for eight years. He had been killed instantly in an accident, and his shocking abrupt passing in the prime of his life had meant it was very difficult for her to move on. We sat opposite one another as I shared what I felt. It was like recalling my own memory, where every detail was in HD. My senses merged as I relayed the information – tastes came to me as words, smells came through as feelings, colours came as smells. Despite this cross-wired download of information, everything that came out of my mouth made sense. I felt his physical pain at the moment of impact, which took me by surprise. I cried tears for a man I never knew, and I shared the most profound and loving experience with a stranger.

It was then I knew what I wanted to do with my life. I had my Calling.

Most of us are programmed by society, our upbringing and our peers to follow a certain path. Yes, there are a lucky few who know from a very early age what they want to do with their time on this planet. I used to envy them when I was job-hopping and wondering where the hell all my gathered random collection of skills and experience would lead me. This will vary from culture to culture but, generally speaking, it involves the tricky process of growing up, finding some way to earn a living so that you can support yourself, and perhaps eventually a family, then keeping your fingers crossed that you have managed to stash away enough cash to support your retirement. For many of us, our childhood dreams do not end up our adult reality.

According to various sources, fewer than 10% of people are living or actively pursuing their dreams, which means that at least 90% of us will never fulfil our life purpose. This is staggering, sad and likely the reason there is so much mental ill-health and unrest in the world.

Kids, as you know, dream big. They see life as a limitless source of opportunity; the possibilities of what they can do or achieve are endless. They have time to allow their imaginations to run wild without the burden of reality to temper their enthusiasm. So why do 98% of people leave their dreams on the cutting room floor of their childhood and depart this planet without fulfilling their truest potential? Oh my God, 98%. Can we all just take a moment here? This is huge. It seems so huge that it can't be real. I don't know about you, but I sure as hell don't want to be part of 98%, and I hope the good news is that you and I don't have to be.

There are three main reasons people don't follow their dreams: time, fear and finances. Jobs, responsibilities, social life, relationships and lack of sleep can all zap our energy and block our inspiration. Rejection and failure are the breaks that stop us from moving towards our dreams, and money is often the deciding factor realising our ambitions. With globalisation and financialisaton an ever-present juggernaut, most of us are simply doing our best to survive, let alone thrive. Before you get sucked in the quagmire of a life without dreams, there is light at the end of this tunnel. Remember there is ALWAYS light if you choose to look for it.

My childhood dream was to be an actor. I have no idea where this came from as neither of my parents had artistic careers. They both had their own businesses and were sporty rather than arty. That said, my mum used to make her own clothes, buying material and copying the latest fashions for a night out with her friends, and my dad played the flute as a kid. Both my papas painted, so there are artistic genes in the family. I remember putting on plays as a child at my grandparent's house in the summer. I have a vivid memory of creating a theatre out of the downstairs hall. It was rectangular in shape with a tiled floor and windows along the whole of the back wall that brought the garden inside. There were plants all along the window ledge, and when it was humid and warm, it smelt like a greenhouse. In the winter, the hall area would have been cold, so my grandparents hung a thick velvet curtain that drew across the bottom of the room separating it from the stairs that led up into the house to prevent the cold air creeping up in the cooler weather. This space made the perfect stage for the audience (my beleaguered grandparents and uninterested siblings). I can't remember if I ever managed to tread the boards in my homemade Broadway, perhaps I have blocked the episode from my consciousness, but either way, it is a dream I pursued until my teenage years. My mum recognised my passion for the arts and lovingly and diligently took me to acting classes as a child, even when I didn't want to go because I didn't like one of the girls in the class (she was a bully and made me feel insecure). By taking me, at times kicking and screaming, my mum taught me about commitment, dedication, hard work, confidence, teamwork and not giving up. Lessons that have stayed with me to this day. They are the fundamental reasons that the arts should be an integral part of the school curriculum and every child's life.

Despite the often excruciating experiences during those acting classes, which included learning how to be a fried egg and playing Postman Pat, I loved it and was cast in a few plays including a panto called *The Decanters of Cultureland* at the Mitchell Theatre in Glasgow where I proudly played the ex UK Prime Minister Margaret Thatcher (this is no reflection of my political leanings, I was just chuffed to bits to have been picked to play one of the leading roles.) I'm still not sure how learning to be a fried egg is the right training for playing a world leader, so if anyone can join the dots feel free to contact me.

I grew up pre-internet, so we entertained ourselves using our imaginations and the latest toy craze. For me, it was My Little Pony, Cindy and roller boots. I also spent a lot of time drawing, particularly horses, which I remember being obsessed with. It was no surprise that I studied art all the way through school and favoured the creative subjects to the sciences. My acting dreams slowly fizzled out as school, exams, hormones and 'what am I going to do with my life?' took over. Before I knew it, I found myself at Aberdeen University studying Land Economics and acting was no more. How did I end up studying Land Economics? A boy.

Having missed out on a television and media course at Glasgow University (the next best thing to drama school), I ended up going into Clearing (a service provided by the UK's Universities and Colleges Admission Service if you didn't manage to secure a place at university or college). Having been bullied for most of secondary school, it was a bloody miracle that I managed to find a boyfriend, so when the choice about what course to apply for came up, I followed my heart and moved to the Granite City (Aberdeen) where he was already studying Land Economics. As it turned out, we split up at the end of the first term, and I was left with a broken heart and a broken brain from studying economics! I managed to stick the course for two years before I took 'a year out' to consider my options. I never went back. Me and economics of any kind, land or otherwise, were never going to be a match made in heaven.

I travelled to Israel to work on a Kibbutz and had an absolute ball despite the ongoing political troubles that plagued the country at the time (and still do). I met some amazing people from all over the world who accepted me for being me. Despite the daily hard graft and scorching heat (I am Scottish and my skin doesn't love the blistering heat), I had one of the best experiences of my life. I grew up and grew into myself on that trip, and it sparked my passion for travel and different cultures. I realised that I had stifled my free spirit for a very long time, and once the genie was out the bottle, there was no way I was going to put it back. After travelling through Israel, I moved to Cairo then on to Paris, where I lived for a year before coming back to Scotland, finding a job and immersing myself in the club scene.

Disenchanted with life as a Sales Exec (no offence, it just wasn't for me), I longed for a creative outlet once again. I found it in dancing and singing, and toured the clubs of Scotland and Northern Ireland, combining my passion for expression with my love of music – and as it turned out, partying. I was a clubber at the height of the 90s, and it was pure escapism, from the drudgery of a 'proper job' and from deciding what I was going to do with my life. I was seduced by the music, the people, the DJs. I felt the music in my body silence past hurts. Strangers felt like lifelong friends as we connected at a higher level. It was like an out of body experience that felt electric and anchored at the same time. I was a free spirit, liberated on that sticky, sweaty, smoky dancefloor, surrounded by kindred spirits. In my element, we shared the same energy, pulsating on the dance floor moving like a musical murmuration. My imagination was once again able to run wild; life was limitless, and anything was possible. Dancing and singing gave me the creative outlet I needed until, one day, I found myself performing in an under-eighteen's nightclub to a crowd of young kids. I remember coming off stage at the end of the set, knowing that was the last time I was going to dance/sing in a nightclub. I realised with abrupt clarity that I'd been running from my past rather than towards my future. I was craving more depth to the friendships I had forged and found the absence of truth an endurance test.

A few years passed before I found myself, once again, longing for a way to express my creativity. I'd been working in various sales roles before landing a job with a radio station, once again in sales. It's difficult to walk away from a job that pays you to have the gift of the gab! They were looking for a new breakfast show and were auditioning for presenters. Despite having zero experience or knowledge of radio presenting (why let a silly wee thing like skills and experience get in the way?), I decided I would throw my hat in the ring. Needless to say, I never got the job, but it ignited something in me that was not ready to be extinguished. I sent off my demo to countless other radios stations and eventually managed to get a six-month stint on a local radio station on the south coast of England. I packed in my full-time well-paid career and drove south. Six months turned into nine, and I was hooked. This was my Calling. I was sure of it. I felt it in my bones. When the contract ended, I drove home, undeterred that I'd been unable to secure another on-air role. On the drive home, I received a call from an old colleague who told me about a two-month contract working for a trial radio station. I rented a house in

Glasgow, interviewed for, and got the job. Days before the end of that contract, by sheer and utter good fortune (or Universal flow), I heard about a full-time presenting job on a breakfast show.

The reason I am sharing all this with you is twofold. Firstly, it lets you see who I am and what makes me tick, in the hope that you see yourself in these words too, but also to remind you that the clues to Your Calling are littered throughout your life, and there is a running theme between all the clues. For me, it was and is communication. Sales is communication, mediumship is communication, acting is communication, radio presenting is communication, art is communication and writing is also, you guessed it, communication. Everything I did was about communicating, whether that was an idea, a product or service.

The mistake many people make, me included, when it comes to understanding our soul's calling or life purpose, is the need for specifics. They want to know exactly what it is that they are supposed to be doing. I certainly did, which was why I missed the signs. This is unbelievable when you look at the definition of communication:

> **communication (n)**
> 'the imparting or **exchanging of information** by speaking, writing, or using some other medium.'

My purpose was staring me in the face the whole time. I didn't see because I was looking for it. This is not new – you've heard of the expression 'can't see the wood for the trees', meaning we are too involved in the details to notice the whole picture. We are all born with gifts to share with the world. These are talents that we use to fulfil our soul purpose.

Or to put it another way:

> *Each of us has been made for some particular work, and the desire for that work has been put in every heart.*- Philosopher-Poet Rumi

Most often, these gifts unfold as a child. They are the things you were passionate about and immersed yourself in for hours on end. Mine started off as a combination of expression and imagination when I used to stage the plays as a child, but ultimately, I was trying to communicate. As a child, our vocabulary is often limited, and our emotional being is underdeveloped or immature, so we struggle verbally to communicate how we are feeling or what we want to say. That's why so many children use art and drawing to express themselves and interpret their life. It's easier to draw what we are experiencing than verbally communicate it – another reason (like we really need it) to make the arts an integral part of all school curriculum.

The Calling is about remembering and honouring your gifts. For many of us, acknowledging that you have a gift, let alone saying it out loud, is difficult. It seems a little egotistical, superior, or at the very least lacking in humility, to think or say, 'I have a gift'. I was put off using the word gift for years because my own experience of the acting, media, mediumship and art worlds was, at times, not that great. So many of the talented people I encountered in these areas did not gracefully share their gifts. Their ego led the charge, and I associated having gifts with being self-centred, selfish and arrogant. Their gifts were the meat (vegan or otherwise) in an ego insecurity sandwich, and I did not realise that until much later on. There is a difference between being egotistical and acknowledging that you have a gift. We also have to acknowledge that ego is a complicated facet of human nature. We need ego, and it's not a bad thing, but when it's out of balance, it can be our downfall.

The reason I never fully embraced the word gift was because I felt it implied that I was special or different from those around me. This was based on my experiences growing up and interacting with those who dined out on the ego insecurity sandwich. With the bullying throughout my childhood, all I wanted was to be the same as everyone else, so embracing this took a lot of work and a lot of time. The truth is that I was and am special, and so are you. I wish I'd realised this a lot sooner, but that was my lesson to learn. Let me set the record straight (imagine a wagging finger here!); we are all special, and we are all different, unique in every way. And that's how it is supposed to be. You know this on the surface, but you need to feel it in your soul. We spend so much of our time on this planet trying to conform and be the same as each other that we miss what makes us all so special. Our uniqueness is our gift to the world and each other, and the more we embrace this, the more we will all grow on this soul journey. Once again, the Universe loves a contradiction and the more we embrace what makes us unique, the more connected and aligned we all become.

I want to explore the notion of *service* or *being of service* because it gets a bit of a bad rap these days and perhaps for good reason.

> **service (n.1)**
> c. 1100, 'celebration of public worship,' from Old French *servise* 'act of homage; servitude; service at table; Mass, church ceremony,' from Latin *servitium* '**slavery**, condition of a slave, servitude,' also 'slaves collectively,' from *servus* 'slave'

Remember the origin of words still reside in our spiritual DNA, so it makes perfect sense that we baulk at this one. Today though, thanks to the wonders of modern language, it has many meanings:

> **service (n)**
> **kindness**, an act of assistance, employment, waiting a table, usage, solution, the armed forces, a ritual, an overhaul or repair, crockery, a sporting term, a writ or summons and having sex.

Considering the last point there, no wonder we're all bloody confused and can't fully commit to the word.

The truth is that everything we do serves others in some way or another, whether we like it or not. Service is an energetic transfer, a flow from you to me, them to us, it to that, etc. It's not a duty; it's a fact of life. We all need what each other has, so we all serve one another. The penny dropped about using the word service for me when I was pulling together a plan for my art business. I was trying to work out who my art clients were, and I was really struggling to work out who might be into abstract

167

spiritual art. Naturally, I hoped everyone could be clients – after all we are souls having a human experience. I wanted to spread the love as far as I could, but in real terms I was casting my net too wide. I researched 'understanding your clients,' mediated on it, asked friends and family who they thought would buy my paintings, and I still couldn't define my ideal client. It wasn't until I heard a podcast that suggested asking 'who do I want to serve' instead of 'who are my ideal clients' that I realised who they were.

Service is not a sexy word (unless you're having consensual sex ☺), but it's what makes the world go around. Even in death, we are still being of service to one another, but that's for a different time or a second book. The reality is that being of service is what makes us tick; it's our purpose. Your Calling is the 'how to' part of getting a kick out of life. It's the meat (vegan or otherwise) in the energetic sandwich of flow from you to me. The best bit about The Calling is that when you are fully aligned with it, expressing your true essence and in complete flow, the wins, losses, gains and do-overs (an inevitable part of life's journey) become part of your story, and you accept them all with the same knowing that they are integral to your gifts.

When reconnecting with Your Calling, try to remember to look for patterns throughout your life, rather than search for specific details. Our calling is how we express our gifts, and that can manifest in many different ways. How you share your gifts with the world is the exciting part…

Chapter 17

The Rising

Not much has been written about what to do after you find peace of mind - or in this case return to soul. This stage is called The Rising. You are bursting with vitality, enthusiasm and determination. How should you harness and channel your new energy?

The Rising is the collective word for this stage in your SuccesSoul journey. I should have called the chapter Your Rising because it is yours and yours alone. However, I trust what came to me, and you will understand why it is The Rising as the chapter unfolds.

Your Rising

What does it feel like to read these words? Your Rising. Take a moment and explore the words. Let them roll around your mind. What do they feel like? Are you sending the energy outwards when you say the word 'You,' or do you claim it as your own? What comes up for you when you say 'Rising'? Does it make you feel empowered, or do you want to keep a lid on it?

Try **'My Rising'** instead and see how that feels.

There are thousands of self-help books on the market because there are thousands of ways to help yourself become who you truly are. However, there is only one rising; yours and yours alone. You are the author of that story. No one can tell you what your life is going to be like except you. The rising is about claiming your story and owning it.

Much has been written and shared about personal transformation, and there are common threads and similar stages to Spiritual Awakening, which is why self-help and spiritual books are so important because they support, inspire and guide anyone ready to step closer to their soul self. Making a conscious decision to embrace all aspects of yourself is opening, unfolding and becoming. The Rising is pure possibility, expansive, infinite (if that doesn't scare you too much) light, truth, connection, knowing, Oneness. The descriptions are endless because The Rising has no limits or boundaries; only the ones you set yourself. Knowing this should not phase you in the way it might have at the beginning of your SuccesSoul journey. You are remembering, and you are reconnecting with your truth.

The Rising is more of a returning (the Universe contradicting again). A return to self. A return to soul – it is SuccesSoul. Given the very nature of The Rising, it would be impossible for me to write a chapter that would speak directly to everyone. I can, however, write a chapter that speaks directly to you, dear reader. You and I are connected through this book; our soul paths were destined to cross because we make a soul contract to help one another in this lifetime. You are helping me share my gifts with the world by buying and reading this book, and I am helping you to reconnect with your soul self – to be SuccesSoul. This energy exchange is pure flow. It is The Rising in action. We rise together.

> As I write the words 'we rise together', I feel a pulse of energy deep in my being. Subtle but powerful, it is pure knowing. I know we are meant to share this journey together, and I can feel as I write these words that we are connected, and we are returning to each other at this very moment. Wherever you are in the world, I see you, I see us, we are One.

Your Rising is as unique, special and precious as you are. Every single being on this planet, billions of souls, all able to rise. All able to reconnect to all that is. All able to live a SuccesSoul life. Can you imagine how different the world would be if we all chose to rise together? That time will come. But this is your story and Your Rising. Like a droplet of water hitting a pool that sends shockwaves outward, Your Rising will inspire others to rise. Not only by sharing your story, but by being your story. For this reason, I chose not to share my rising with you. You don't need the distraction. You need a clear heart and mind to access your own inspiration. What I can do is guide you to harness and channel your new-found spiritual energy, which is now flooding your being and is the fuel for Your Rising.

You have to rise or return on your own. It is destined to be this way, not to test you, but to inspire you to voyage into the depths of yourself to find the present that leads to your future. To find the story of your life.

I hope you are buzzed and excited by the possibilities that lie ahead. I know I was. I had no idea where I would end up, but for the first time in my life, not having a plan was the best plan I had. Simply reconnecting with Your Calling has the power to centre you and trust that you are on course. It is liberating without feeling like you are freefalling.

There are three parts to the rising, common to everyone, irrespective of their stories.

Imagination. Connection. Action.

All good stories start with imagination. It is the catalyst, the power that will take you straight to possibility. Without connection and action, imagination will remain a daydream hanging in the gallery of your mind.

Most people use the word imagination to refer to creativity in the sense that someone has a great imagination or no imagination at all. Or they use it to refer to picturing something in your mind. But imagination simply allows us to explore ideas that are not in our present environment or even real. Humans take information from the outside world, such as light, or sound waves, and find meaning in it, using memory and perceptual processes. Imagination works in reverse. Imagery is created from our memory. We can use our imagination in the same way to access our soul memory, so it is irrelevant whether you think you are creative or not – as an aside EVERYONE is creative, but that's another story.

Just as our bodies hold memories of everything that has ever happened to us in this lifetime, our soul memory holds experiences too. All of our experiences are recorded somewhere in our physical selves, but not just in this lifetime. If we think of the soul as the eternal part of us that will continue on long after we leave our bodies, it makes sense to think that our soul must have been doing something before it came into our body as well. Our souls have history and hold the key to our future. So, when I say you have to use your imagination, I mean you have to access your soul memories.

Accessing soul memories using your imagination takes a little practise, and there are lots of different ways to help you do that, from meditation, yoga, running, anything that takes you out of yourself and into yourself. You could try past life regression, Shamanic or energy work. Sometimes just doing nothing is the best way to release your memories. There is no right or wrong way of doing it. You will be full of vitality, enthusiasm and determination to lead the life you came here to lead. Sometimes we have to step out of the way of ourselves to let that happen. When we do this (and leave behind our preconceived ideas about our lives), we enable flow, and opportunities often present themselves that either come out of nowhere or seem too good to be true.

This was such an amazing time for me. I had connected with my Calling and felt I knew what the outline of my story was – communicate in some form or another so that I could activate and inspire people on their journey. I wasn't entirely sure what it was going to be, but it would be creatively based. Without forcing or chasing opportunities, I found them quite by 'accident'. I wasn't looking for anything in particular, which left me open to possibilities. Often our Calling is not what we thought it would be or we have different callings at different times in our life. If we do have different callings, there will be a running theme to them. Your Rising is about allowing the flow of opportunity into your life.

Connection is the next 'stage' in Your Rising. It is when all the disparate parts come together to form a whole or one truth.

> **connection (n.)**
> late 14c. conneccion, 'state or fact of being connected, also connexioun (in this spelling from mid-15c.), from Old French connexion, from Latin *connexionem* (nominative *connexio*) 'a binding or **joining together**,'

This happened fairly naturally for me. I wasn't aware of *doing* something, and I only realised I was past this stage with the benefit of hindsight. This stage is about trust and being the vessel for all the composite parts to collect and blend together. The less you do here, the more things happen. To connect, you have to sever your involvement in the process. Connection is also about attraction, of the people, places and experiences that support you on your soul path.

And finally, action. **Action is flow in motion.**

I have talked about not trying to force or chase anything, which might seem contradictory when I tell you to take action. But taking action is doing something to achieve a goal. You have the end result or an aim in mind and therefore, a framework to work with. Forcing is overdoing it. This lacks the subtlety and balance of action. Chasing is scattergun, kind of like a hamster on a wheel, heading nowhere because you have no aim in mind.

When you act upon (taking action) your connection, which has been inspired by your imagination, you are rising. This is The Rising.

Chapter 18

Your Future

This closing chapter brings together all the stages that you will have gone through reading this book, the purpose of which is *How to be SuccesSoul*. By now, you will know what that means, and it will resonate with you at a deep level. Your Future is about *you* and *your* story. Only you know what happens next. However, there are a few tips I can share to help attract the future you desire. I have also left a few pages at the very end of the book blank and invite you to write your closing chapter; today, tomorrow, in two years' time.

When I first decided to write this book, I considered how it might culminate. I didn't want it to be an anti-climax or leave you hanging, or worse still, have you needing to reach for another self-help book because this one was no help. I want this to be a guidebook or a vital tool to help you find yourself – kind of like a spiritual orienteering compass. For those not familiar with orienteering, these compasses differ from normal hill-walking type compass in a number of ways but an essential feature is quick dampening of the needle so that it becomes steady as soon as you stop at a track junction to take a bearing.

Each chapter has been designed to represent different compass points on your SuccesSoul journey. Each stage in your unfolding is a different track junction, and each chapter helps you find your way. It is vitally important to me that you do find your way home, that you reconnect to your soul because once you truly do that, you will not need help trying to fix what was never broken in the first place. I am genuine in my heartfelt wish that you feel reconnected enough in yourself that you are able to answer the questions that will inevitably arise as you navigate the rest of your life.

I want to remind you that *How To Be SuccesSoul* is not a quick fix. It does not promise to magically change your life overnight. It is not a 'heal yourself in thirty days', or a 'zero to hero in five easy steps'. It is a guidebook, a spiritual manual to help you on your journey where the destination is You. It will support you in reconnecting with your soul.

This journey will undoubtedly feel bumpy at times. You will be knocked off course, and you will suffer disappointments and hiccups along the way. But they will not blindside you in the same way they did before. You will absorb them into you. Think of this book as more of a spiritual gym programme where you commit to building strength for maximum gain. Each chapter gives you advice and insight to help you get stronger, so you're better able to shed your old self and reach your soul self, lighter than you were at the beginning. And just like the orienteering compass needle becomes steady as soon as you stop at a track junction to take a bearing, you too will be steady when your life hits a junction.

Ok, ok, enough with the analogies! But, hey, a good analogy is the best way to say what we have to say sometimes! Anyway, you get the picture.

By now, I hope that you know what it feels to be SuccesSoul. You may have read this book over a period of time, taking each chapter and stage at your own pace, and that's great. You may have consumed it in one sitting or even fast forwarded to the last chapter – I sometimes do that with a new book so no judgement I promise. How you ended up here is not important, knowing what SuccesSoul actually *feels* like is.

SuccesSoul is being **near to** your soul. It is blending mind, body, soul. It is becoming whole or one again. It increases your wellbeing. It is stability and trust. It is the glue that keeps everything together. It helps you grow and learn. It is connection and togetherness. It is a relationship, and it is the most important relationship you will ever have.

> **relationship (n)**
> 'sense or state of **being related**,' from relation + -ship.

It is coming together, returning home, the peace and serenity that has been missing. It is timeless, un-wanting, caring, moving and flowing. It is ease, here but also there, now and then; it is stillness and it is travel. It is joy and tears, creation and destruction.

destruction (n.)
early 14c. from Latin destructionem (nominative *destructio*) 'a pulling down, destruction,' noun of action from past-participle stem of *destruere* 'tear down, demolish,' literally '**un-build**,'

It is feeling and being, together and alone. It is sensing and intuiting, releasing and holding on. It takes and it gives, hangs on and lets go. It is a continual moment of pure bliss that fills you with so much love that you want to leave everything and disappear.

disappear (v.)
early 15c. *disaperen*, 'cease to be visible, **vanish** from sight, be no longer seen,'

It is belonging, intimate, rejuvenating and empowering. It is sacred, being found, significant. It is hope and faith, knowing and believing. It is outward and inward, vast and minute. It is a realm that is both here and there in the same moment.

realm (n.)
late 13c. '**kingdom**,' from Old French *reaume*, probably from *roiaume* 'kingdom,'

It is honouring, harmonious, restful and vital. It is connection and isolation, familiar and unknown. It is freedom and joy, inexplicable and profound. It is sublime and intoxicating, ecstasy and enchantment.

ecstasy (n.)
late 14c. extasie '**elation**,' from Old French *estaise* 'ecstasy, rapture,' from Late Latin *extasis*, from Greek *ekstasis* 'entrancement, astonishment'

It is all of these experiences, feelings, knowings and senses all at the same time – they are One.

Why did I include definitions of words most of us know, and their past and present meaning? Coming at it from a different perspective, perhaps our struggle with verbal communication is the result of only having learnt to recognise and label with words the feelings we are familiar with? It would be fair to say that we struggle to accurately articulate new sensations because we don't know the word for it yet. We feel more than we have the vocabulary to articulate and express, which is in itself profoundly frustrating. People work through feelings by being able to identify them and use them as signals.

It is imperative that we expand our vocabulary to support our reconnection with soul. As we become more aware of our feelings, we are able to shift the way we feel. To become more aware of them, we have to be able to label them – with words. Words help us to identify and articulate our experiences, and they form the basis of our connection to one another and ourselves. If I was a gambling woman, I'd wager most of us take language and vocabulary for granted, perhaps only noticing its (or our) limitations when we find ourselves unable to express ourselves with words.

A quick aside; expressing your feelings can make you feel vulnerable, and you may worry that telling the people in your life how you feel could drive them away. There is also a technical term for a difficulty in identifying and describing emotions – alexithymia – which is someone who has trouble defining and explaining how they feel. For example,

181

they struggle to put anything more complicated than basic emotions – sad, happy, mad – into words. This is different from a limited vocabulary.

Currently, there are roughly six and a half thousand spoken languages in the world today, and two thousand of those have fewer than one thousand speakers. This seems way more than is necessary, but I am thankful because I have found the words that help describe the sensations of being SuccesSoul and listed them in the section below. Who knew that somewhere on the other side of the world someone was using a word that I would find to describe my own personal experience? I told you our uniqueness was our gift to the world.

Dr Tim Lomas has created the positive lexicography, an evolving index of 'untranslatable' words related to wellbeing from across the world's languages. Dr Lomas, you ROCK! His TEDx talk *'Expanding our experiential horizons through untranslatable words'* explores how untranslatable words – terms without an exact equivalent in our own language – can expand our horizons and transform our lives. Dr Lomas believes these words have the potential to help us better understand and articulate our experiences and can even reveal new phenomena which had previously been veiled to us. BOOM!

'As we become more aware of our feelings, we are able to shift the way we feel, and to become more aware of them we have to be able to label them – with words.'

So, without further ado, and with gratitude and deepest heartfelt thanks to Dr Lomas, (and the many souls across the globe speaking these languages), here is what soul reconnection or SuccesSoul feels like:

Dadirri (Australian aboriginal) – a deep, spiritual act of reflective and respectful listening.

Sukha (Sanskrit) – genuine lasting happiness independent of circumstances.

Gigil (Tagalog) – the irresistible urge to pinch or squeeze someone because they are loved or cherished.

Iktsuarpok (Inuit) – the anticipation one feels when waiting for someone, whereby one keeps going outside to check if they have arrived.

Yuan bei (Chinese) – a sense of complete and perfect accomplishment.

So… now that we know what SuccesSoul feels like, and it resonates with you at the deepest level, what the hell are you going to do now?

Million. Dollar. Question.

I. Don't. Know.

'What???? I've come all this way, and that's the ending?'
No problem expressing yourself now is there? ☺

I don't know because I don't have your answer. I have my
answer. Your future is about You and Your story, not me
and mine. Yes, our stories are now woven together
forever, connected thanks to this book, but you don't
want my life any more than I want yours, and I can only
give you my life story. No offence meant by that, I simply
mean we each have our own wonderful journeys to make
in this life, and you came here to experience yours not
mine. The good news is I can help you find it. The better
news is that you are already nearly there – you are
SuccesSoul.

There are infinite possibilities to connecting with Your
Future. I cannot possibly list them all – even if I could,
you'd get bored reading it. What I can do is share with
you some of the things I did, as well as some of the
things I feel guided to tell you about. This list is not
exhaustive, and you do not have to do everything on it.
The best way to approach this, and to tackle life in
general, is to be present, to be open and to expand into
the possibilities. Take a moment to centre yourself and
connect with your higher self, your soul self, before
reading the list. When you do this, you are balancing
your energy and igniting your spidey senses. We
connect with Universal wisdom through all of our senses
and sometimes these merge, so you taste words and
smell feelings. This sounds confusing, but it feels
perfectly natural. I find it helpful to imagine, or visualise,
my energy expanding outwards like a forcefield. You

might feel a subtle tingling sensation in your body, so send that feeling out in all directions. If you don't sense it, this is okay too, just set the intention that you are open to receiving. Once you feel ready, you can read through the list and something will pop off the page for you – trust what that is. Your own spiritual compass is directing you.

A footnote except not at the foot! Connecting with Your Future can make you feel anxious. It can be a frustrating, challenging, scary, lonely and confusing experience. *'Shit really?'* Yep! But you know what, you are prepared for it. You are not the person you were when you started this book. You know that divine light is on your side and divine light beats the crap out of anxious, frustrating, challenging, scary, lonely and confusing so… **Bring. It. On.**

Let me tell you something, you would not have gone to the bookshop, or found the online store, bought or downloaded this book, read it and come this far in your journey to SuccesSoul living if you were not ready for Your Future. You are ready, and you've got this. I know you know this, but I'm reminding you – in case you have a mini wobble, which you might, but that's okay too. Wobbling only serves to remind you how stable you really are – if you weren't, you'd fall over and that ain't happening. **Not. On. My. Watch.**

For anyone who has a wobble about remembering Your Future (and you are remembering because you were born already knowing, you have just forgotten), I ask that you transform that energy (feeling) into inspiration.

185

inspiration (n.)
c. 1300, 'immediate influence of God or a god,'
especially that under which the holy books were
written, from Old French *inspiracion* 'inhaling,
breathing in; inspiration' *Inspire* (v.) in Middle
English also was used to mean 'breath or put life or
spirit into the human body; **impart reason to a
human soul**.'

How do you do that? Two ways, and you know what the
first one is by now...

Words.

There is a reason that words and language have been an
integral thread in this book. You should, I hope, know by
now that words have a profound or limiting effect on the
way you live your life because of the effect they have on
your soul. Words are vibration and sound (energy), and it
is the vibrations that create the reality that surrounds you.
If you have ever explored The Law of Attraction, you will
know this to be true. Everything you say is a
manifestation. Without words, we have no thoughts, and
our thoughts become our reality. Words are our most
powerful asset, so use and choose them wisely. Instead
of telling yourself you are anxious or (insert other fearful
word), tell yourself you are inspired. All of the feelings
above stem from fear and that fear is a lack of belief in
soul self. How can you be SuccesSoul and have fear? You
can't.

The second way to stabilise your wobble is colour.

Colour.

As a mediumistic and intuitive artist, colour is always my starting point. I connect with the energies of each colour and use them to communicate Universal activating energy, guided by Spirit and my own soul. Colour healing or Chromotherapy has been used for millennia to balance and enhance the body's energy centres/chakras by stimulating the body's rebalancing process. The ancients built great halls of colour healing, where individuals entered and were bathed in light that was filtered through various coloured glass panels or windows.

Colours are wavelengths of electromagnetic energy, scientifically proven to promote physical and mental health and wellbeing, reduce stress and alleviate pain. Simply staring at a blue painting, for example, has been proven to have an immediate calming effect, lowering blood pressure and the heart rate. Red, on the other hand, has the opposite effect; it stimulates the sympathetic nervous system, speeding up heart rate, and increasing blood flow and blood pressure. Recent research, focusing on the psychological and physiological effects, has shown that visual art interventions reduce distress, increase self-reflection and self-awareness, alter behaviour and thinking patterns, normalise heart rate, blood pressure and even cortisol levels. **

One of the easiest ways to connect with the transformational energies in colour is to really look at the colour and allow the feeling (their energy) to wash over and through you. You can try it now by looking at this square of four colours: turquoise, magenta, orange and indigo help rebalance and can support you in feeling less fearful about Your Future.

Start with whichever colour you are drawn to first, and when you feel ready, move on to the next one. You can also look at all four colours at once and take in all their energy at the same time.

So, what do these four colours do?

Turquoise increases your intuition and sensitivity and relaxes sensations of stress. It helps with intellectual and intuitive insights and renewal.

Magenta strengthens contact with your life purpose. It is magnetic so attracts spiritual power and life path.

Orange is cheery and frees up the body and mind. It also stimulates creative thinking, enthusiasm and helps assimilate new ideas.

Indigo is freeing and stimulates the third eye (pineal gland), which increases clarity, concentration and intuition. Indigo also governs physical and spiritual perception.

Talk about the fab four! If these energies don't supercharge Your Future connection, nothing will. And, just for good measure, the number four resonates with the vibrations and energies of devotion, practicality, endurance, stability, passion and drive, so say 'Hello' to Your Future, people.

I would suggest saving images of these colours onto your mobile. You can look at them whenever you feel the need. You can also use colour as your computer screensaver to get a wee fix while you're at work. Try it. I promise you won't be disappointed.

Stepping into Your Future

So now that you are inspired by the possibility of Your Future, how do you step into it? The following list includes the steps you can take to Your Future.

Stop.

Open.

Listen.

You were expecting more, weren't you? It's not always slog, slog, slog, you know and as De La Soul once sang, 'Three is the magic number.' This principle is also captured neatly in the Latin phrase *omne trium perfectum*: everything that comes in threes is perfect, or, every set of three is complete. It's also a writing principle that suggests that a trio of events or characters is more humorous, satisfying, or effective than other numbers, but I'm not using it for effect. There are only three things you need to do to become Your Future.

Stop. Open. Listen.

Stop...

trying. Where do I start with stop trying? First, let me make a disclaimer. I am not suggesting you sit on your arse, do nothing and expect the world to land in your lap. This is not a fairy tale people, it's real life, and in the real world that is never going to happen. What I mean is stop forcing life to happen. Stop trying to control or manipulate or juggle or trade to make shit happen. Just let it happen to you, not by you. Easier said than done, I know.

Humans are hard-wired to control everything – you can take the person out of the cave, but you can't take the cave out of the person. From an evolutionary point of view, if we are in control of our environment, we have a far better chance of survival. As Homo Sapiens, we learnt that if we controlled our surroundings, we might avoid being met by a grisly fate. That stuff sticks. Even now, three hundred thousand years later, we are still trying to prevent a grisly fate from befalling us. If you're honest with yourself, your entire world is about control. But don't worry, we are all in it together. You are not alone.

> **control (v.)**
> early 15c. countrollen, 'to check the accuracy of, verify; to **regulate**,'

When we try to control anything or anyone, we are trying to regulate or find balance. It's difficult for us to shake the innate desire to control because it's not just us trying to control our little corner of the world. The physical world is controlling us too. Take the laws of physics and gravity, for example. A force that tries to pull two objects towards each other. But what a very weird, if not momentarily exciting, experience life on earth would be if we were not forced to stay on terra-firma. The weather or its personification, Mother Nature, is another example of control. I appreciate we are influencing the weather with climate change, but as a force, we cannot control it. Manipulate yes, but control no. A simplistic way of looking at things, but you get the picture.

Control is ultimately about trust, which I touched on in Chapter 7. Stopping is not about downing tools and waiting for a miracle, it's about trusting that a miracle will happen. So, when I say stop, I mean trust.

Open...

up. Your heart, your soul and your mind. When you are open, you are curious. You seek out new people, places and experiences. Being curious is being open to seeing what happens. It's not about a predetermined path or outcome, but about receiving. It is welcoming and inviting, setting the intention for attraction. Be less judgmental of yourself and others. This is hard because it is in our nature. However, we are all doing the very best we can with what we have in this moment. Opening your heart is having compassion and empathy for yourself and others. We all suffer at some points in our lives, and there is no pleasure without pain. You must remember that when you are on a pleasure wave, someone else may be on their pain wave. Be creative and express yourself. There are many ways you can do this through art, craft, word, music, dance. Creativity is the very expression of soul, and it can be a moving meditation, so find a way to connect with source and express yourself. And the superpower to being open and SuccesSoul is gratitude.

> **gratitude (n.)**
> mid-15c. 'good will,' from Middle French gratitude (15c.) or directly from Medieval Latin *gratitudinem* (nominative *gratitudo*) '**thankfulness**,' from Latin *gratus* 'thankful, pleasing'

Gratitude is one of my favourite words and so fucking powerful. I promise you. (Sometimes only a good swearword drives a point home).

Practise gratitude every day.

It is the fastest route to SuccesSoul living, and the ripple effects can be felt by everyone around you. If you don't know how to practise gratitude, here's how:

Start small and build it up. Feeling is the key here; don't just say the words, *feel* them. When you're in bed tucked up for the night, take three deep breaths and relax into yourself – don't fall asleep! Say in your head at least one thing you were grateful for in the day, even if all you can muster is being alive – no matter how bad things get, life is a gift. Don't just say, 'I am grateful for being alive', feel it. Draw your attention to the centre of your body and feel the words as you say them. If you can smile when you are saying them, it helps shift the energy. When you wake up in the morning say (feel), 'I love my life.' When you go to bed at night practise gratitude again and add something or someone else to your list. **Sleep. Eat. Repeat.**

Listen...

to your heart's calling, to the voices within you. Listen to your angels and your guides. Listen to the friends and family who know you best and whose opinion you trust. But most importantly, and above all else, listen to yourself because you already know all the answers. You have to get out of the way and allow the wisdom to arrive. Listening is not just about hearing, far from it, in fact.

This holds true when we listen to ourselves as well as others, which is interesting given the significance of language and vocabulary as a tool to understanding ourselves and our surroundings.

When we are communicating with others, pitch and tone of voice, speed and rhythm of the spoken word and the pauses between those words express more than what is being communicated by words alone. Gesture, posture, pose and expression usually convey a variety of subtle signals as well. It is the same when we communicate with ourselves. When we listen to ourselves, we are listening for the subtle signals, not just the words rattling around in our mind. We are listening to our internal reference point, with which we should always be in touch, our inner consciousness, our soul.

Our soul speaks to us through all of our senses. I have said previously in this book that when we connect with Universal wisdom, that which is our soul, we can taste words or smell feelings. Our soul communicates in this way, which is why, for example, your intuition is often communicated as a gut feeling. Listening, by definition, is paying attention to sound. Sound is energy. Listening to our soul is paying attention to our energy.

> **attention (n.)**
> late 14c. 'a giving heed, active direction of the mind upon some object or topic,' from Old French *attencion* and directly from Latin *attentionem* (nominative *attentio*) 'attention, attentiveness,' noun of action from past-participle stem of *attendere* 'give heed to,' literally **'to stretch toward**,'

Of the three steps toward my own future, Stop was the most powerful, rewarding and aligning. In relinquishing control of a preconceived outcome, you open yourself up to infinite possibilities, often resulting in opportunities or a course of action that you had not previously considered.

One of the biggest challenges we face in flowing into our future is our requirement for security – financial, emotional and biological. Society is structured in such a way, and we are conditioned in our thinking and behaviour to provide for our future selves based on our present circumstances. This is not only an ever-evolving process, but it is also a very limiting way of approaching our own personal evolution because it does not consider our spiritual selves, only our mind and body. We can override this conditioning by trusting. Trusting that you are exactly where you are meant to be in this very moment. Trusting that you have all the answers. Trusting that the Universe has your back. Trusting that everything you are experiencing (good and bad) is exactly what you are meant to be experiencing.

> I was guided to study Soul Plan a few years ago, which is a new interpretation of an ancient system of life purpose analysis. Derived from ancient texts, such as the *Zohar* and the *Sefer Yetzirah*, which explore the creation of apparent reality through sound, letter and word. Soul Plan also includes a method of gematria channelled by Dr Frank Alper 1930-2007 in his *Spiritual Numerology of Moses* work. The Soul Plan system interpretations have been modernised and expanded by Blue Marsden who has also channelled additional material highlighting the theme of non-duality.

I believe, and Soul Plan is centred around the belief, that we are born into this life with a soul blueprint, a plan for what we are here to experience. We *chose* this plan and are born knowing this plan, but as we move through childhood and live more fully in our human bodies, we forget or disconnect with this plan. We may experience inklings or flashes of knowings and rememberings throughout our lives, but for the most part, we are detached from it unless of course, we choose to reconnect. This choice to reconnect is what you are doing by reading this book and becoming SuccesSoul.

When you reconnect to soul, when you choose to be SuccesSoul, you are no longer passively moving through life. You become the creator, activating your life. It is the single most important act of love you can do for yourself, and it will take you from existing to living.

* www.lexico.com/explore/how-many-words-are-there-in-the-english-language

** US National Library of Medicine

About Vicky Paul

Photo Credit Zeno Watson

Vicky Paul is an intuitive, artist and writer who creates to activate the soul. Inspired by the invisible space between mind and body that connects us all as human beings, she is passionate about deep transformation and human potential.

Always a free spirit, Vicky grew up in Scotland, drawing, writing, listening to music, dancing and acting, knowing that creativity and communication would be part of her future. She enjoyed a successful career as a multi-award-winning radio presenter, interviewing many of the biggest names in the industry, from Kylie to George Michael and Madonna, before a profound experience left her able to sense and work with energy. Vicky took workshops at the world-renounced college of spiritualism and psychic sciences, Arthur Findlay College, with James Van Praagh, an American author, teacher and spiritual medium and June Field, a gifted Scottish medium crowned the 'World's Greatest Psychic'. Vicky is also a qualified yoga teacher, energy worker and most recently trained in Soul Plan, a powerful and accurate system of life purpose guidance, spiritual counselling and healing.

As an artist, Vicky is intuitively drawn to the energies in colour, instinctively combining paint and mixed media, adding dimension, texture and layers to bring the canvas to life. Stylistically diverse, her work invites you to reconnect with the awareness behind your thoughts and emotions and delve into the mystical side of life where true meaning is found. Vicky's paintings have been shown in galleries in London and Edinburgh and are part of private collections in the UK, Japan and Canada.

Vicky is driven by her desire to raise vibrational awareness and nurture our connection with soul-self. *How to be SuccesSoul®* is Vicky's first book and was written with loving guidance and channelled wisdom from her Spirit Guides, Archangel Michael and Archangel Zadkiel.

With Gratitude

So many people have played an integral role in my SuccesSoul journey, and for that I am truly grateful. From family and friends, to strangers and mentors, you have inspired, guided, motivated and grounded me towards a life of meaning and purpose.

To Junie June, my beautiful mum. You are an inspiration. Thank you for teaching me about myself and about life, for encouraging me leap and catching me when I fall, for giving me your laugh, and reminding me that I can be anything I choose to be. You introduced us to spirituality and opened our minds to the possibility that there was more to life than what we could see. You have always been my champion and my biggest fan, even when I shouldn't have given up the day job!

To my beloved husband Ford. My love. My partner. My rock. Thank you for loving me the way you do, for always encouraging and supporting me to express myself, for giving me the grace and space to be myself and for inspiring me to be a better person. I love being on this adventure with you.

Daddy. Thank you for encouraging me to stand tall, for pushing me out my comfort zone and for showing me that we have to live life to the fullest. You epitomise the law of attraction, even though you don't know it, and are more spiritual than you care to admit.

To my wonderful 'step-mum' Leigh. Thank you for showing me grace and diplomacy in action, for teaching me that the loudest voice is not always heard first and for all your guidance, support and love.

To my beautiful skin n blister Lisa. You are my right hip, best friend, partner in crime and wise counsel (aka leveller!). Thank you for reading the first draft of my book, retaining your enthusiasm for a story you've heard a thousand times and for guiding me to make the right changes.

To my big bros David. Thank you for inspiring me to look outside the obvious, for sharing your superior intellect and for showing me that bonds cannot be broken, despite time and distance's best effort.

To my in laws, Derek and Ada. Thank you for being such wonderful, supportive second parents. I love being part of your family.

To Team Fam. Thank you all for the very best times, for the honesty, belly laughs and high jinks, and for showing me that friends are family. Here's to the commune, it's closer than we know.

To our wee dog Lucy. You are a humanimal, my constant companion and the embodiment of unconditional love. *Weee dog*.

To my publisher Sean Patrick at That Guy's House. Thank you for giving my book wings and letting my story fly. You have made one of my dreams come true and for that I am eternally grateful. Let's change the world one page at a time.

To my editor, Clare Coombes at Liverpool Editing Company. Thank you for giving me confidence in my writing, and reminding me that it's ok to let go.

Thank you to the team at That Guy's House; Lee Philpotts for your patience, creative eye, design skills and for bringing my ideas to life, Marianne Morrisey for your eagle eye proofreading my book and Arinze Ikeli for your patience with the typesetting.

To Lynette Gray. Thank you, thank you, thank you for connecting me with my publisher. I love watching your bright light and boundless energy. Keep shining.

To Juliette Knight. Thank you for reading and editing my very first book proposal, despite the ridiculously tight turn around! You gave me the confidence to send it, and for that I am very grateful.

To my friend, mentor and kindred spirit Helen Jones. Thank you for your support, guidance and continuous insight. You gave me the confidence to own my gifts and continue to inspire me with yours.

To Jessica Vesterlund, you are an inspiration and one of the wisest women I know. Thank you for seeing into my soul and showing me how to show up.

Thank you James Van Praagh, June Field, Jennifer Starlight and Lorna McLean for helping to free my soul and show me what I am here to do. To the teachers at Arthur Findlay College, and to Peter Urs Aeberhard and Florence Botté, thank you all for keeping my spirits up, making me laugh and sharing such a magical life changing experience. To Blue Marsden, Sarah Lermit and Andrew Cooper-Knight for teaching me Soul Plan and to Jacqueline Adams for my first reading. Thank you to Elaine Thorpe and your Guide for reconnecting me with my painting.

Thank you to Jason Stephenson, for your magical mediations and silky voice. You're letting go and surrender meditations oose compassion and empathy and have been a huge support to me during my awakening.

Thank you to Dr. Tim Lomas and Sebastian Gendry for giving me permission to include some of your work in this book.

To my clients, supporters and social media followers. Thank you for allowing me to share what is in my soul, and for supporting me as a creative.

To Archangel Michael, Archangel Zadkiel, my spirit guides, ancestors and papa. Thank you for your constant whispers, lessons, activations and healing. You have shown me the meaning of true beauty and have guided me to a place of trust.

And most importantly, my wonderful readers. Thank you for listening to your soul and showing up on this journey. We are forever connected and I am humbled that you have read my story.

With so much gratitude and love. Xx

Things I Love

Books

You Can Heal Your Life, Louise L. Hay (Hay House, 1984)

The Celestine Prophecy, James Redfield (Warner Books, 1993)

The Power of Now, Eckhart Tolle (Hodder & Stoughton, 1997)

The Alchemist, Paulo Coelho (Harper, 1988)

Soul Plan: Reconnect with Your True Life Purpose, Blue Marsden (Hay House, 2012)

The Desire Map, Danielle LaPorte (Hay House, 2012)

Light Is The New Black, Rebecca Campbell (Hay House, 2015)

Podcasts

Under the Skin, Russell Brand

Super Soul Conversations, Oprah

In Daily Breath, Deepak Chopra

People

Jason Stephenson
Instagram and Facebook: @JasonStephensonMeditation
YouTube: youtube.com/user/ILoveJuicyShow

Lisa Gerard
Facebook: @LisaGerrardOfficial
YouTube: youtube.com/user/LisaGerrardChannel

Karunesh
Facebook: @karunehsmusic
YouTube: youtube.com/user/KaruneshWorldMusic

Mei-lan Maurits
Instagram: @meilanmaurits
Facebook: @MeilanMauritsRise

Snatam Kaur
Instagram: @snatamkaurkhalsa
Facebook: @snatamkaur

Deval Premal
Instagram and Facebook: @devapremalmiten
YouTube: youtube.com/user/PrabhuMusic

Terry Oldfield
Facebook: @TerryOldfieldMusician
www.terryoldfield.com

Esther Hicks / Abraham
YouTube: youtube.com/user/AbrahamHicks
www.abraham-hicks.com